SECOND START

W9-CAA-046

SECOND START

Paul Salsini

Our Sunday Visitor, Inc.
Huntington, Indiana 46750

Copyright ©1980 Our Sunday Visitor, Inc.
All rights reserved. No part of this book may be reproduced or copied in any form or by any means — graphic, electronic, or mechanical, including photocopying, recording, taping, or information storage and retrieval systems — without written permission of the publisher.

ISBN: 0-87973-525-2
Library of Congress Catalog Card Number: 79-92442

Published, printed, and bound in the United States of America

525

Acknowledgments

This book could not have been written without the help of the priests who opened their doors and their lives to me. To them, my sincere thanks. I would also like to express my deep gratitude to Tony O'Brien, for his lively encouragement and assistance, and to my family, for their support and endurance.

—P.S.

Table

of

Contents

SECOND-CAREER PRIESTS

Second-Career Priests:
They Heard the Call

Peter and Andrew, of course, were the first. The fishing was fairly good on the Sea of Galilee, and they were satisfied with their work. They had comfortable lives, enjoyed their families, and yet, when they heard that irresistible call — "Come, follow me!" — they immediately put down their nets.

In the long history of the Church since that day, countless others have put down their nets, their tools, their pens, their instruments, leaving one career for another, this time to do God's work. Some became aware of the call only gradually, subtly. Others, if not knocked off a horse by lightning, received the call to priesthood suddenly and dramatically.

But there is a new and little-noticed phenomenon in the Catholic Church. More and more men are entering the priesthood later in life, many of them after successful business or professional careers. With the predicted shortage of priests in the next decades, second-career priests seem to be one way, however small, to help fill that gap. But, more than that, with their varied backgrounds and life experiences, they are bringing an exciting new dimension to the priesthood.

The movement is so young, in fact, that it doesn't yet have a name. In gathering material for this book, I found several ways to identify this new breed of priests. *Late, delayed,* and especially *retarded,* vocations, however, seem to have a negative connotation — as if the prospective priest arbitrarily put off his decision or, as one seminary teacher said, "the Holy Spirit got lost on the way." *Adult vocation* is somewhat closer to the mark, but that term is also used for the growing number of young men who enter a seminary soon after college, without any notable work experience. *Second-career priesthood* seems to be the most appropriate, especially since it gives the priesthood the professional image it requires and deserves.

Whatever the term, more men are entering the priesthood later in life, some at thirty, some at sixty, and everywhere in between. They have been greatly encouraged by the establishment of two seminaries specifically designed for older men. No one has figures on the number of second-career priests — because no one is keeping track — but it may be significant that while other seminaries are noting sharp declines in enrollment, these two places are recording increasing numbers of applications and admissions.

The older of the two, Pope John XXIII National Seminary in Weston, Massachusetts, was founded in 1964 by Richard Cardinal Cushing of Boston. Although it is underwritten by the Boston archdiocese, Pope John Seminary welcomes men from throughout the country. In 1973, Sacred Heart School of Theology in Hales Corners, Wisconsin, operated by the Sacred Heart Fathers, began a program for second-career diocesan priests, along with its traditional training for members of its own order. In addition, Holy Apostles College in Cromwell, Connecticut, which previously welcomed older men for pre-theology training, began its own theology program in 1978. Religious orders are also initiating programs for the older vocation, and "traditional" seminaries are noting an increase in the average age of students.

The movement, of course, parallels events elsewhere in society. Career decisions in general are being made later in life; and such decisions need not be permanent. Much has been written about mid-life changes and the desires of men and women to start new, sometimes entirely different, careers. With more people switching careers, those changes have become more acceptable. Priesthood, however, still has a mystique about it, and people wonder: "Why would a man, successful in his career, leave all that to become a priest?"

The conversations I had with second-career priests give several answers. Again and again, many men would speak about "the call." Often, the desire to become a priest was there since childhood. In fact, many second-career priests had, when they were young, started on the traditional road to ordination by entering a seminary after high school. They found, however, that they had too many doubts about themselves and their vocations, and they left. But that desire resurfaced at some point in their work experience, and they yielded to it again, this time as more mature individuals, better able to make the decision.

For a few, there were specific "religious experiences," some of them dramatic. While those who have not had such experiences may question their validity, even psychiatrists have found that there can be such occurrences. And certainly the Church recognizes that God's message can suddenly and clearly be heard. But more than such an experience is necessary for a vocation. Father Peter Conley, academic dean at Pope John Seminary, says: "We certainly accept religious experiences as distinctly possible. If we didn't, we wouldn't be in the right business. But we have to watch out — how had this man performed in the past? How has he continued to perform after his religious experience? What are his social relationships? How does he hold his job? These are a better measure of the Holy Spirit."

There are other influences. Priest models from childhood or, later, as friends, are considered important. Religious readings have attracted some men: note in the following chapters how Thomas Merton's *The Seven Storey Mountain* continues to shake the souls of those yearning for God.

For all of that, there appears to be a single, clear answer to the question "Why did you want to be a priest?" Service. Vatican II, of course, stressed priesthood as service to the People of God, and this appears to be the major attraction for second-career priests. Father John Cain, vice-rector at Sacred Heart, says:

"Ninety to ninety-five percent of the people who come here are here because they want to serve God's people. The other five to ten percent are not as clear, and they see the priesthood as security, as a priest of the 1940s. They quietly make the discovery of what the priesthood is, and they leave."

And, Father Conley adds: "Roman Catholicism doesn't believe in the 'Baby Jesus, come and squeeze us' kind of theology. The God that we see and experience through the sacraments comes only for people. So, therefore, if we're going to be men of God, we're going to be men of the people."

Many second-career priests have been in service-oriented professions (although Sacred Heart once had a man who formerly washed elephants in a circus). It is a logical extension for a man to serve people as a teacher, a social worker, a lawyer; and then to serve the People of God as a priest. Almost invariably, however, there was a feeling of some unfulfillment in the previous career, a desire for an elusive "something more."

"Most of the men who come to us are successful — if they are failures, we'd want to know why," says Father Cain at Sacred Heart. "They've had a successful business, very good income, financial security, good clothes, good apartments, cars. But it still did not satisfy them. There was something missing and they were looking for it. They got beyond the material and started searching for the spiritual."

The fact that they are "searchers," however, has caused some concern. In interviews, I found bishops and vocations directors wary of the motivation of those who were not satisfied in one career and turned to the priesthood. Seminaries that train older men are well aware of the possibility that the priesthood might be sought as an escape and a refuge, and they have instituted psychological tests to determine motivations. At Sacred Heart, for example, a psychologist has found that a man seeking a second career as a priest is fundamentally "one who has not yet developed a firm sense of his own identity but is engaged in the active search for it."

Searchers, however, can be dynamic and valuable people. They can provide a vitality for people who are also searching.

Father Conley says: "In the extreme case of the searcher, we would say no. There has to be a little bit of the found. But I like to think that if someone feels the call to the priesthood, he is searching for God. I like that element." It's rather exciting to think that a priest and his community can take part in that search together.

In a Church that is so strong in its traditions, of course there is some reluctance to break away from the age-old system of mainly seeking young men for the priesthood. The Second-Career Vocation Project, established by the Marianists at the University of Dayton (Ohio) in 1977, has found that bishops need considerable coaxing to accept older vocations. As a result, Father William Ferree, its director, warning of the coming crisis in priestly numbers, comes armed with statistics.

The figures are formidable. While the Catholic population of the country was increasing from 47.9 million in 1969 to 49.8 million in 1978, the number of priests declined from 59,620 to 58,485. That kind of decline might not seem too worrisome until one looks at the number of students in seminaries: in 1969 there were 33,990; in 1978 there were 14,998.

Many seminaries have started active recruitment programs for younger men, but Father Ferree says that the crisis is so near that a priestly time bomb will go off in the next decade or two unless older vocations are also encouraged.

There are, of course, other answers: women priests or married priests are obvious answers to the numbers problem, but the Church thus far has turned aside those solutions. The Church has, however, instituted a permanent diaconate program and has encouraged more active participation by the laity in liturgical and parish affairs.

But second-career priests should not be considered simply as so many pegs to be put in so many holes. Second-career priests have an obvious advantage in serving the People of God. They bring to their priesthood years of experience — in careers, in community involvement, in dealing with people, in relationships with women, and perhaps even in family life. In short, they have experienced life. Those who argue for a more prominent role for second-career priests say these experiences help them bring Christ to the people and help the people more easily identify with the priest. No one says that older men necessarily make better priests, however; what they do say is that those who have such desires should be encouraged.

In the following chapters, second-career priests tell their own stories. You will find a lawyer who now works with an inner-city education agency in Illinois; the former head of an employment service working in campus ministry; a former securities executive who is now a hospital chaplain; a jazz musician at a parish in Connecticut; a former vice-president of an ad agency at a midtown Manhattan church; a former policeman serving a parish in Georgia. And more.

They trace their lives and careers, their accomplishments and frustrations before entering the priesthood. They describe how they decided to become priests. And they tell of the joys and the fulfillment they have found in priesthood. The reader will note that these men are all very human, with frailties and anxieties shared by all of us.

Although each man is different, some common themes seem to run through their lives. Many were unable to come to grips with the call for years. They seemed to have the ability, as one says, "to deflect the Lord." Even though most were successful, they recognized that something was missing from their lives, and found it in the priesthood. Some painfully broke off relationships with women. But all say that they are happier and more fulfilled now that they have put down their symbolic nets and made a second start.

JAMES HINCHEY

An Activist Meets New Challenges

"It seems so implausible now, but I could not decide to decide about the priesthood. I could decide about everything else, I was a take-charge person. I never just sat around wondering what I was going to do with my life. I think I always thrust myself into pretty creative activities, and I was always on the move. I think one way I deferred making the decision was that I was always in process. I'd say, 'Well, when I finish this, I can face that.' Finally, I realized that I was never going to be finished with everything."

Friends of James Hinchey, who agree that he is indeed a take-charge and in-control person, find it hard to believe that it took him a dozen years to decide to enter Pope John XXIII Seminary. He had been en route to priesthood before, but he was only twenty then, and it was for a monastic life, which he came to feel was not right for him.

In the intervening years, Hinchey grew out of what he calls the "Catholic-ghetto life" of his childhood. As a college English teacher, he observed the student unrest of the sixties. The John Kennedy years made him politically alive, and as a social activist, he was involved in a voter registration drive and sit-in. Hinchey also ran for public office, and he learned of the needs and concerns of other peoples through extended visits abroad in the Experiment in International Living program.

It was in the Umbrian hills of Italy that he finally made his decision.

Born in Omaha, Hinchey spent most of his life in the Midwest and now is in Brooklyn, New York. Only a couple of years after his ordination, he was made administrator of St. James Cathedral, the mother church for the Brooklyn diocese. It is an exciting place, moving away from the traditional territorial parish into a community and liturgical resource for Catholics from throughout the area. Hinchey finds it interesting that in his life before priesthood he went out to people abroad. Now he is in the diocese that is the first home for the continuing wave of immigrants to this country...

I always say I grew up in a Catholic ghetto. This was in Detroit, where we moved when I was in the first grade. I thought I was very urbane and sophisticated, and perhaps in a limited sense I was, but I really didn't know much about realities that weren't white and middle-class and Catholic. I had virtually no Protestant friends. I went to Catholic elementary and prep schools and all of my associations were Catholic. It really was the time in the life of the Catholic Church when life revolved around family, friends, and the church.

I think we were a pretty ordinary Catholic family, not pious. I tried to corral them into saying the rosary in October once or twice, but found that wasn't such hot stuff. My father was a daily Mass-goer and communicant, though, from the time I can remember, and that has been a very subtle influence. He was never somebody who laid this on anyone else in the family; he simply got himself up at six o'clock and went to Mass. But if you were to meet him, you would not regard him as a pious or extremely religious man.

From the time I was an altar boy, I had some thoughts of priesthood. In high school they became more prominent. I was captivated by the idea of monastic life, but there were other attractions too — the contemplative life, teaching, missionary life.

All those things drove me crazy because they all seemed so attractive. I regretted that I didn't have the single-mindedness of some of my friends who not only knew that they wanted to be doctors, but brain surgeons. I wanted to do it all. But I never wanted to be a diocesan priest. In fact, when I grew older, I had disdain for the diocesan priesthood. I thought the religious life was the ideal expression of the priestly commitment.

After a year and a half at St. Benedict's College in Atchison, Kansas, I entered Gethsemani, the Trappist monastery in Kentucky. During high school I had made a couple of retreats there. In fact, I met the novice master and had quite a long talk with him. I didn't realize it at the time, but it was Thomas Merton. I felt really blessed that I was able to interact with him naively. It was a splendid experience.

Later I got to know Merton well. He was our spiritual father; I felt I could tell him anything. Merton was one of the most human persons I've ever met — great sensitivity and compassion and a wonderful sense of humor, especially in the pre-Vatican II Church, in a monastic community where there was real austerity and absolute conformity to the great regularity of life. He was a real breath of fresh air. I think of that passage from Isaiah about not breaking the bruised reed or quenching the flickering wick — that was the sensitivity he brought to novices who he sensed were having a difficult time or needed special kinds of attention. And he was one of the most faithful and regular monks in the monastery. He did all of that, was the master for thirty novices, came to choir, gave special conferences, and frequently went out to work with us in the afternoon.

Gradually, I felt that I had to grow and develop in ways that at that time I wasn't certain I could do in a monastery. I became almost obsessed with seeing the world, with learning. At that time at Gethsemani the importance of learning was downplayed. It was very difficult, but I decided to leave.

So I went back to St. Benedict's and completed college studies there. At that point, I decided not to decide.

I was an English major and when I graduated, I applied for a couple of fellowships. I thought, "If one is offered, I'll take it."

That was an example of not really making a conscious decision but allowing somebody else's decision to become mine.

Well, I was offered a teaching assistantship at Duquesne University in Pittsburgh, and I worked on a master's degree there. Once you get onto that academic track, there seems to be an inevitability about it. Naturally I went on for the doctorate. I had a couple of offers and chose the University of Wisconsin. But I found that I didn't have the mentality or the disposition to be a scholar: I wanted to be a teacher. After finishing the preliminary exams, I heard about the University of Cincinnati offering teaching positions for those without dissertations. And the money sounded decent, so I wrote and was hired.

Something else was happening to me at this time. I became politically of age. I think all of us came alive when John Kennedy was running for president. I remember going to Kansas City in 1957, when he was still a senator, and hearing him speak and shaking his hand. At St. Benedict's, I remember having people in my room watching the Nixon-Kennedy debates. At Duquesne everything would stop if Kennedy had a press conference. I remember in 1962 he came, and I waited two, two and a half hours to get a seat.

I was in Madison when he was assassinated. I couldn't imagine that there would be anything as shattering as that. There was a deep anger and bitterness, a sense that we had to grow out of a more innocent world. While I thought I was very much in touch with human frailty, my own and the world's, I never dreamed that we could be that dark. And Kennedy remains one of my great heroes. All of the efforts to demythologize him don't make me feel any differently, because I believe in what he stood for. I was in Poland in 1963, and when I think of the way some of the Polish intellectuals spoke of Kennedy, it only reinforces my opinion that he was probably one of the greatest influences in the world in our time.

Another part of my blossoming, if you will, was getting involved in the Experiment in International Living in Putney, Vermont. The idea was that people learn to live together by living together, so they sent students to live with families abroad. If enough people did that, they thought, there would be peace and understanding. I think it had great impact.

Well, I applied for such a scholarship from the Experiment and they sent me to Italy the summer of 1960. I think that revolutionized my life. I came in contact with students from all over the country, people filled with excitement and hope. It was an awakening for all of us. I came back determined that I would see the rest of the world. Then I applied for something more exotic. I figured that since I'd been in Italy, I could go to India; and I did. In 1963, I lived in Poland and Russia; in 1965 I went to Israel.

While I was doing this academic thing, an extraordinary part of my life was this other movement. It opened my consciousness to realities about other people, what the human heart longs for — understanding, an opportunity to grow. I think I was brought in touch with the spiritual longing of people, especially in a country like India, where there was a totally different cosmology and a different religious orientation. Politically, it made me aware that there aren't good guys and bad guys.

In 1965 I went to the University of Cincinnati as an instructor and taught there for four years, all the while knowing that I had to finish the dissertation. I taught senior-level courses, and that was a wonderful experience — courses in American literature and drama. These were English majors who were very serious about their studies, and it demanded a lot of my time.

At the end of four years I knew that I wasn't going to finish my dissertation in that setting, so I went to Italy for a year as director of an independent-study program for the Experiment. I thought I could finish the dissertation at the same time. It was while I was in Italy that the whole idea of priesthood really came into focus again, and this time it seemed it wasn't going to go away. I hadn't been able to come to grips with it because I didn't want to give up what I had. I wasn't very trusting in the Lord at that time. Or in myself.

At that time I began thinking of the diocesan priesthood. When I came back to Cincinnati, I saw the vocations director and even took a couple of courses at the seminary. But I guess I just wasn't turned on by the situation I saw there.

And then I got this terribly attractive offer: I had a chance to go to Urbana College, in a town of twelve thousand in south central Ohio, outside of Springfield. I would be teaching, have a chance to shape programs, be in charge of the English program; and there was a small drama program. I thought, "Wow!" Then, too, the college was tottering on the brink of disaster, and the fact that this was a make-it-or-break-it thing appealed to some instinct.

I always had a way to deflect the Lord.

So I went to Urbana in the fall of '71, and it was a good experience. I bought a big house in the country, a humongous farmhouse, filled it with four or five friends who were connected with the college, and we had a sort of utopian society.

And then I became very, very involved in some political issues. The idea of serving ... I thought the idea of priesthood was connected to the idea of serving, of being involved in things that would change the quality of life. And I thought you can do the same thing in politics. I still have that idealism, but I think it's as difficult to effect change in ministry as it is in politics.

So I got involved in some voter registration issues over whether students had the right to vote where they were attending college. Court decisions had been handed down saying that they did, but the local figures in Urbana said that they didn't. Students were very exercised about it, and they wanted to know whether there would be support. I went to talk to the local officials, but they didn't want to hear anything about it. They felt threatened by the way students might vote. We said, "Well, you can't deprive people of that right; it's been clearly established." So we sat down at a polling booth and we were all arrested. It turned out to be a tempest in a teapot, but it generated a lot of angry charges — that we were irresponsible and that we were interlopers. They said crazy things. You know ... that we were Communists. Unbelievable! But in the midst of all that, there was a lot of healing; and, believe it or not, a lot of the people who were saying those things subsequently supported my candidacy for the state legislature a few months later.

John Gilligan was governor then, and his office was looking

for plausible candidates to run for the legislature on the Democratic ticket. Well, they heard me talk a couple of times, they knew about my involvement in the voter thing, and I had met the governor a couple of times. I realized I was bait being thrown to the barracudas. This was in the Seventy-fifth District. The Republican incumbent had been in office for twelve years and also happened to be speaker of the house. "Well," people said, "if you don't win this time, you certainly will the next time out." And there were moments when I really thought I was going to win. In fact, I got about forty percent of the vote, which was marvelous. I mean that was damn good.

It was the year that George McGovern ran for president, and while I had great admiration for him, it was not the best time to be running for a Democratic seat. Some people thought I might soft-pedal my support for him, but I said I couldn't do that, although I knew it wouldn't help an already difficult campaign.

It was an exhilarating experience for me. I loved it and I felt like I did it well. I loved getting up in front of a group and fielding questions. That was an ambiance I felt I held my own in. We had a lot of volunteer help, a lot of students at the college. I wasn't able to afford radio time or billboards, but I went to every speaking engagement — the Lions, the Rotary, school boards. We had the *Hinchey Report,* a planned quarterly newsletter that I would have sent to constituents, and we did three or four of them during the campaign. We had a letter-writing campaign. We even had a group called Republicans for Hinchey.

I should say that at this point there was a very close friend of mine, and we had a profound attachment to one another. We'd talked about marriage on any number of occasions, and now we were talking more seriously. But then I had this utterly clear realization of what was happening. I hadn't resolved the idea of priesthood at all. I was running in a thousand directions to try to avoid it. And now I was not only going to do myself irreparable harm but somebody else real harm too.

So we broke our engagement. It was very painful. We had known each other for a long time; and, though I'd been talking about the priesthood since the first time we met, she thought it had dissipated. She had doubts herself about marriage. It really boiled down to the fact that you can't make this kind of commitment and involve yourself in another person's life if you don't feel sure about it. And as painful as this was, it would have been infinitely more painful later.

So I plowed headlong into the campaign ... and lost.

When I lost, I was disappointed and relieved at the same time. It meant that my future was unclear—if I had won, I would have known what I would be doing. But it also meant that I had to get down to the business of sorting out something about my interior life.

I planned the summer quarter in Italy with a group of students. I thought, "Well, I'll come back to Urbana one more year, and *then* I'll go into the seminary." In some ways I was still putting off the decision.

Well, in Italy I had the closest thing to an illumination, if you will, of what I was doing and what I needed to do. I had taken the group to Assisi, which was always a favorite place of mine. I remember taking off by myself to the mountain hideaway of St. Francis and going to Mass there. The Gospel was the one in St. Matthew in which Jesus says "Come, all you who are burdened." It was a zinger. Even though I had heard it a thousand times, all of a sudden it just said to me ... well, what was I concerned about? Why was I so reluctant to give it a chance?

And then I went down to San Damiano. There was a priest there and I sat down with him and he started to tell the story of Francis and his vocation and his struggle. He said it was probably a very hot day, very much like that day, and this young man who was very popular, very romantic, and had this great sense of being alive, was tormented and distraught, and came down here almost on the verge of a breakdown. It was as if the story was brand new. It brought tears to my eyes. I thought, "Whew, that's what I'm going through!" I started to leave because I was supposed to meet the students, but as I went up the mountain I suddenly thought: "This is the dumbest thing in the world. I want to go back and hear the rest of the story." So I turned around and ran back.

I know this sounds like a small incident, but it was very important to me at the time.

And at that moment I knew that I was not going to delay any longer. I knew that God was asking me to trust Him. If I tried and it didn't work out, my life wouldn't be over. But if I responded generously and it did work out, how much richer I would be for it: I'd be at peace.

When we got to Florence, I sent a telegram resigning my job at the college. Then I called my parents and told them. My parents are wonderful. I think they long since stopped being surprised by what I do.

I decided not to wait another year. I went to Pope John XXIII Seminary for interviews and was accepted for the next semester.

I was thirty-five when I entered the seminary and thirty-eight when I was ordained in '76. You know, I fear that if I had completed the studies when I first went in and entered the priesthood, I might not have stayed. The question of maturity is an important one, and I think it takes very stable and mature decisions before one enters the priesthood. I know what kind of changes I went through as a person during that period; I would have gone through the same changes as a priest. I can't imagine my leaving now. I think that's because I know that there is disappointment and failure and a sense of incompleteness in every life. But there are also vast possibilities in every life, and I really believe that the Lord provides us with what we need to be faithful to the promises we make.

My first assignment was St. Martin of Tours in Bushwick, which is probably one of the most devastated areas in all of New York. After being there a year and a half, I came here to St. James as a result of a proposal I made to the bishop. I didn't expect him to say yes so quickly. I guess he recognized that my life experience counted for a lot and maybe even was equivalent to x number of years in the priesthood. So I came here as part of a team and then was named administrator.

The cathedral was virtually dormant. It hadn't been active. My proposal was that we make it truly a cathedral, a pastoral center that would draw alienated, disenfranchised Catholics, give them a sense of community. I had proposed that we focus on liturgy, fine, excellent liturgy, and adult-education programs. Then the cathedral, as mother and teacher for the diocese, would be an expression of the best pastoral outreach that the entire local Church could offer. That's what we're trying to do.

We're not doing anything revolutionary, but we're trying to celebrate liturgy well and with integrity. I guess anybody can say that, but often their budget belies it. We're trying to be faithful to that in the way we allocate the little money we have. We also place great emphasis on the quality of preaching. It is just impossible to get up in front of well-educated, hungry Catholics and give them pabulum. The kind of Gospel we're preaching is that all of us are called to create a kind of kingdom of justice, before which there can be no peace. No world peace, no peace in the city of New York, where we all worry about being mugged and raped and burned, and no peace in the family. We can't talk about world peace until we talk about our most immediate relationships.

I guess one of the things that's different about me now is that in the sixties I felt I had to go out and conquer the world. I know now that we do that by understanding our relationships with the people who live around us first. One thing we preach a lot is that it is not possible for people of faith to live the Gospel just by coming to Mass and saying x number of rosaries and novenas; that unless we are coming to celebrate an experience that we have, maybe it is even questionable whether we should be called a eucharistic community.

My priesthood is constantly full of surprises. One aspect that I'm trying to to contend with—and I think this is a difficult thing for all diocesan priests—is the tendency for your life to be fragmented. I find it important to choose how you define your time, how to say no and not feel like you're a bad priest if you say no. Because otherwise you find that you're divided into ten thousand pieces every day, and no human being can survive that.

There are many satisfactions. I think one of the great things for me — another aspect of the priesthood that I couldn't have sustained twenty years ago — is knowing that I don't have to be the one to care for everybody else, that I can allow myself to be cared for by others. I think there was a time when priests couldn't be cared for; and it's a beautiful thing to know that while priests have a very clearly defined role and people have legitimate expectations of priests, the people also have a ministry to them.

There are some aspects of priesthood, something of what priesthood is and means, that defy description. A sense I sometimes have is that it certainly is something larger than me, something that transcends the person, the particular gifts: you are a representative of Christ.

I wanted to be a priest because my own training and background, my own Christian formation, led me to believe in the value of service that was Gospel-motivated. I believe that God calls all of us to serve in different ways. I never saw priesthood as sacrifice. It's not a case of giving up everything. In fact, I think the Lord calls us to live lives that will help us to grow in the fullest. And be happy. And I guess what I always wanted to be was happy.

HENRY BRENNAN

A Family Man

"I still think about my wife a lot. I pray for her many times during the day. I pray that we can be together for all eternity. And I believe this will happen. I believe that my wife has been instrumental in what has happened in my family — and there has been so much good that has happened, including my becoming a priest.

"We used to pray every day that one of our sons would have a vocation to the priesthood. So guess what? As my daughter was saying: 'Yeah, Mom always wanted a son who was a priest. Now she's got a husband who's a priest! If she only knew!' Aha!"

Henry Brennan laughs, a hearty outpouring that bubbles up out of his solid girth. His ruddy face becomes redder, making his fringe of a beard appear even whiter.

Father Brennan sits in the pastoral care office at St. Joseph's Hospital in Milwaukee, chain-smoking small cigars and reflecting on his life. At sixty-six, he looks back on a career as a successful businessman. He knew the foot-weary work of a salesman, but also the heady satisfaction of big commissions. He has enjoyed the warmth of a large Irish family and loves to tell stories about his children and grandchildren. He has suffered through a double tragedy and become a stronger yet humbler man because of it.

Now, when other men his age are golfing in retirement, he works upwards of seventy hours a week as a chaplain. In 1977 he was ordained a priest in the Order of St. Camillus.

Henry Francis Brennan, Jr., was born January 7, 1912, in Newark, New Jersey, attended schools there, and went to Fordham University for a year and a half. He dropped out because the money ran out; it was 1932. In the fall of that year he married Agnes Patricia DuBois, the sister of one of his best friends. He was twenty, she was eighteen...

The first part of my business career, if you can put it that way, was in selling hair tonic. And I sold chewing gum, I sold automobiles, I sold beer. As a young guy, I had developed a pretty good pitch. People who didn't have money to buy bread— I would sell them hair tonic. I was a good salesman. Still am. I have a big ego. I think that probably humility is not one of my prime virtues. To be successful in business I think you have to have some kind of an ego. You have to believe in yourself. Maybe that's a better way of putting it.

I sold different things, and then in 1940 I got into the insurance business. I had no training, so I just got a rate book on life insurance from one of the companies and found out how much fire insurance cost on furniture and automobiles and went around and just solicited. Eventually I built up a pretty fair general insurance business, and I sold a fair amount of life insurance.

I was an agent for three or four fire and casualty companies. I guess I put most of my life insurance through John Hancock. I was considered an agent of theirs.

I had a lot of tough years. And I'm not crying the blues. Tough years in the beginning, especially the first twenty. I found an old stub of a check from John Hancock the other day. I had had a good week that week; the stub showed that I made a dollar and seventeen cents. Aha!

Having been in the life insurance business, the natural collateral seemed to be the securities business. Primarily, what I was interested in was mutual funds. I was fairly successful in that, so it was natural that I got into selling stock. At that particular time the market was good, so a good percentage of the stocks that my brokerage house was handling went up. So I was making money for my customers and a few dollars for the house, and I was making a few dollars for myself.

I was living fairly well, but not high off the hog ... not at that time. All of this happened over a long period of time, from the forties well into the sixties. It was in January of '69 that one of my sons, Robert, who is a CPA — I think he was twenty-five at that time — joined me in the securities business. We opened an office in Hightstown, New Jersey, and worked very well together. Business really boomed. It was about the next year that he bought out the firm we were working for. Then a couple of years later we sold that firm and started another. He is a very aggressive businessman, and we started opening more offices.

The newspapers have said I was making a six-figure salary. I don't like that. I'm not denying it; I'm not affirming it. I had a very comfortable income ... very comfortable towards the end. I had some good, real high-commission jobs. Very truthfully, though, I never made the big money, the real big money, until my son Bob came into the business. I was doing all right, I had a new car every two years, and we took a lot of trips, my wife and I. Like every third week we'd take off maybe a week or ten days and go away. We liked to go up to New England, particularly up to Vermont, and we took all the kids, or five kids, or two kids, or whoever wanted to go and could get out of school. Or we'd go down through the Carolinas, and it was just enjoyable. My competitors used to say, "Don't you lose business when you go away so often?" I'd say, "Yeah, I do." But now most of my competitors are dead! Aha!

We had nine children. We lost one at an early age, eight months. He was a mongoloid baby. It was years later that my wife told me that her grief was not so much for herself as it was for me. I guess that's the way love works. I knew how sick the baby was. I used to hold him and rock him and ... I guess she really felt bad for me. Of course she did for herself too.

And then Kevin, of course, we lost.

In May of '69, Kevin, age twenty-three, was working for a large life insurance carrier, working the medical market, and we thought that he would be much better off working for us. We had already started another firm, Princeton Professional Services, Inc., and we made him an offer to be vice-president of it. He hadn't started with us yet, but he had been given a dinner one night by his former employer and was coming home about eleven-thirty. Three sheriff's dupties, who in New Jersey are political appointees and whose primary duty is court attendance ... well, since each one gave a different story as to what happened, I'm not sure really what the true story is.

One said they were alongside him on the road and he was weaving. Another fellow said no, that wasn't so, they were stopped at a light. And I believe they said he looked like a known drug pusher. I really don't remember what the third fellow said, but it was an entirely different story.

They were in an old, beat-up car. Two white men and a black man, in casual clothes, no lights on the car, no siren. They do concur that they told him to pull over. We've always felt that he thought he was going to be held up. He had some eighty dollars on him when he left the dinner; but when the ambulance picked him up, he had no money on him at all. I'm not saying they robbed him first. I don't know. Which doesn't make that much difference. But, anyhow, they shot at him. Poor Kevin! He must have been scared stiff. I'm sure he thought he was being held up.

The whole back of his car was riddled with bullets. They never hit his tires, they never hit him. He thought he could get to our house quicker than his own. Well, he did get to our home, but he never had a chance to get out of the car. There was a starter's pistol in the pocket of the car and somehow he got it out — that's another mystery — and he pointed it at them and the one fellow just fired a shot and blew his brains out. It was right in the driveway of our home in Union, New Jersey.

This was on a Saturday morning. We buried him on a Wednesday morning. Hundreds of people were there. That

Saturday night my wife and I went to confession and ... ah ... we came home and ... ah ... I guess about one-thirty, two o'clock I heard her get up, and then I heard her fall. I could hear that death rattle, and I knew she was dying. I picked up the phone and called the police. They said they had a car right by our house. Evidently they were taking precautions. They were there in less than a minute. But I knew she was dead.

Ah, well ... what more can I say?

There was an inquest into Kevin's death, a long-drawn-out affair. I don't even know what the official determination was. There were editorials and stories in papers all over the country. One paper did a survey of police chiefs and asked them if they were in Kevin's circumstances, would they have stopped their car, and each one said no.

We tried to harbor no ill will for the three men who killed two people. In fact, my family and I still pray for them and their families because they're also God's children.

From what I know and from what people tell me, I guess I took the deaths well. Certainly I was shook — two deaths in a week! I just worked harder than ever, I just kept plugging, I could have killed myself, too, working. I guess I was a little bit numb for a couple weeks. I didn't get mad at God, though there's nothing wrong in getting mad at God in situations like that.

I just immersed myself in work so deeply that it was only when I got home that I had a chance to think.

And I just kept praying, thanking God for all the good things. We had been married thirty-six and a half years. We had a good, loving relationship. One of my sons gave an interview to a paper in Jersey: he said his father thought his mother was the most beautiful woman he ever saw.

And she was very beautiful, beautiful in all senses, beautiful of feature and beautiful of soul and spirit. We had made it a rule that we would never go to sleep without making up after an argument, and we didn't. And sometimes the arguments got hot and heavy, but they were always settled before we went to sleep. I have some letters from my wife — cards, poetry. I keep them in my apartment, and I read them all the time.

30

So now I have seven living children: four sons and three daughters — all married except my youngest, Sheila. And I have twenty-five grandchildren. I thank God every day that I have such good children and such good grandchildren. I'm not much of a letter writer, but I call them all the time, every week or ten days.

Let's see ... there's Henry Francis — they call him Hank like they call me Hank — Michael Dennis, Robert Emmet, Terrance Joseph, Patricia Maureen, Eileen Marie, and Sheila Mary. We got Mary's name for each of the girls.

My wife had six miscarriages, incidentally. And when my oldest son was a kid, he got the mumps and then I got them. He wasn't sick; I was sick. After the mumps, I was sterile — at least I thought I was. Well, all right. The months roll by, the years roll by, no more babies came along. I felt kind of bad about it, I guess my wife did too, but we had four kids then. And all of a sudden one day she said, "You know what?" I said: "You don't have to tell me. I know. You're pregnant. I don't believe it!" She used to say every time: "You don't mind, hon', do you?" "Terrific!" And I used to grab her and hold her and kiss her and she'd kiss me. And four more came along.

I don't want to make any kind of pronouncements on birth control because sometimes I have ambivalent feelings. I can understand the situations where sometimes it would be morally wrong to have more children. I don't know whether the moral theologians would agree with that or not, but I don't give a hoot. And that can go on the record. For my wife and me, to have sex, to love, and to preclude the possibility of having a life formed would have been repugnant to both of us. That probably sounds, well, peculiar today, but that's the way we felt. For me and my wife, to practice birth control would have been morally wrong.

Now, what can I tell you about the children?

Well, there's Pat, the oldest daughter. She can't have children, so many years ago she decided to act as a foster mother for handicapped children. She's had all kinds, all colors, all shapes, all degrees of disability. She's really a tremendous girl.

She has two adopted children. There's Tommy, in grammar

31

school, and Jimmy, who graduated from high school and is now a paratrooper. He has a very high IQ, but he didn't want to go to college right away because he was bored stiff with high school. We were on the Boardwalk in Atlantic City one time—he used to like to go with me because we both have a weird sense of humor. Kind of that Irish thing, you know. Anyhow, I was interested in the black holes in space and started describing them, and he says, "Oh yes, Grandpa, you know how that works..." and he goes into a ten-minute dissertation, giving me all the technicalities. I thought, "Oh boy, why'd I ever bring this up?" Aha!

Sheila ... for the last few years Sheila has lived with Pat and her husband. She loves babies and kids and has a tremendous way with them. Once we had a little black baby, Sonia, big wide eyes — and God, did we love her! We had her about a year, maybe longer. Anyhow, one day Sheila had to take her to the doctor's for a checkup. Sheila is quite light, blonde, and she has a weird sense of humor too, like all of us. So they're sitting in the waiting room and everyone is looking, you know, and Sheila is smiling and smiling. This woman could contain herself no longer and she comes over and says, "Pretty baby!" Sheila says, "Yes." "Is that your first?" the woman asks. And Sheila says: "Yes. But I'll tell you something. I'm going to sue that hospital for three million dollars because I don't think this is my baby!" Aha! She came home and told us that, and we were in stitches. Aha!

Three and a half years ago they took in this seven-week-old baby, interracial, and Catholic Charities named him Sean. Now Sheila has gotten permission to adopt him. He's my twenty-fifth grandchild. He's a very loving little boy, and he gets along well with his cousins, you know. He loves Uncle Robert, and he'll have all kinds of love and support for his life.

And then there's Eileen, a housewife. She's such a prayerful person. When I need special prayers for a patient, I call Eileen first. And son Terry, a CPA and a partner in a CPA firm. And Hank and Mickey, in the financial field and doing very well.

Well, getting back to me, in '72 my son Bob was really running things, and I start taking off sometimes on Thursday afternoons. Drive down from Hightstown, New Jersey, where we had our office, to Atlantic City, check into a motel. I loved strolling on the Boardwalk and, being naturally nosy, an inquisitive and gregarious guy, I got to know quite a few people. I'd walk the Boardwalk, take a book of poetry or a prayer book, sit down every once in a while and read, pray, just meditate. You know, look at the ocean. And then I'd come back on Monday morning. After a while it got to be I'd be coming back on Tuesday morning — which made a heck of a short week of working. Aha!

I really didn't think seriously about the religious life, though, until about January '73. I was sixty-one then, an old codger. I had never, never thought about it before. Not even as a kid.

Truthfully, I think the Holy Spirit was shoving me for a while and I was just ignoring the Spirit. All I can tell you is that something happened one day driving home from the office. *Zap!* — I guess that's the word for it. But I can't describe it. I remember there was a little forest I had to drive through, and suddenly the whole thing came on me. Just like everything came down, you know? *Who was I? What was I doing with my life? What was I accomplishing?* I didn't know what was happening, I grabbed the wheel, I almost went off the road. I was perspiring profusely. Then I started to analyze what was happening. It wasn't, you know, that I should study for the priesthood. It was this sudden focus on my life.

I'd always prayed. I was never a man of great prayer, but prayer was part of my life. After that I started to pray more and ask the Spirit to guide me. The Spirit started to drive me little by little. So I started to think, "Gee, I must have a vocation to the religious life." I started to write to various orders. I called my secretary in one day and I said, "Take a letter. Dear Fathers and Brothers: I am sixty-one years of age, a widower, very successful businessman, interested in your order. Please send literature." She said, "That's some letter." Truthfully, most of them didn't even answer, which teed me off.

But the Order of St. Camillus did answer. They had a hospital and a monastery near Whitinsville, Massachusetts, and they suggested that I might want to visit there. So I got on the phone and, in May of '73, I went up there. Boy that was a hot week! I missed my nice air-conditioned office! They gave me a room in what they laughingly called the monastery, which must have been built about the time Washington crossed the Delaware. It had one window ... up on top. I thought, "It's going to be a great life." I sweated through that. But I guess they sent a good report into Wauwatosa, Wisconsin, which is the headquarters of the North American province. So I drove out to Wauwatosa — I guess it was September of '73 — and I met the people there. I liked what I saw, and I guess they liked me. But I think the top dogs were a little bit skeptical about my age. I said I'd come back.

In November of '73 I booked a flight out of Newark. While I was packing, I started to have second thoughts: "What the hell am I doing? Sixty-one years old and starting a second career? I could take life easy. I could travel around the world, I've got a couple of dollars, business is good. And I don't know if I'll be able to stand the gaff, going to school. This is crazy!"

So I called up and told them, "Gee, I can't make it today." But I'm smart enough, from the business world, to leave the door open: always leave yourself an option. "I'll be in touch with you very shortly," I said. I called the airlines and canceled. But then I went into the kitchen and I really prayed. I belonged to a charismatic group, and I prayed the way they do, asking the Holy Spirit that if I really had a vocation, to let me know. Call it psychological, call it anything you want — I got zinged. So I got back on the phone: "I'll be there tonight."

They decided I could come, though somebody told me later they didn't think I could last two months, maybe not even two weeks.

I came out to Milwaukee and took some courses at Cardinal Stritch College first. Then I went to Sacred Heart Seminary in Hales Corners. I'm not the most brilliant student, so I had some difficulty in some courses, though I got my share of A's and B's. Since the two deaths, my recall has been lousy. The doctor told me the mind cannot selectively block things out, so it blocks everything out. Anyway, I was ordained in April of '77 and started work here at St. Joe's in June.

I picked the Camillans because they are service oriented, taking care of the least of God's children, the sick. Truthfully, I wanted to get into prison work, but I was turned down. I guess they figured I was too old.

The Camillans take four vows: poverty, chastity, obedience, and service to the sick.

Poverty? Well, for tax purposes I'd been divesting myself of various interests over the years, and I really didn't have that much in my name. I had a couple of dollars. What I had, what remained, I just divided up among some of the children.

This life-style in some respects is comfortable. I eat good food, have a nice apartment. I was never much of a guy for clothes. My wife was always after me. In Atlantic City, we'd go into a store, and I was always buying her clothes, because I knew she loved clothes. But she'd maneuver me around to the men's department: "Look at those nice suits." I'd say I didn't know about suits. "You're a businessman, you're successful, you're supposed to be making money, you should wear nice suits!" Aha!

Chastity? I could say I had no difficulty with it, but that wouldn't be honest. I find it difficult. I guess I always had a strong sexual urge; I don't know if it's stronger or weaker than anybody else's. It's still there, and I have to pray and fight about it all the time. I will say that, in the last year, it's become easier since I've been ordained. I don't know why — maybe I make more of an effort. I think God does give us the ability to live a celibate life.

But, truthfully, I'm still too in love with my wife to have sex with anyone else. I couldn't even take another woman in my arms. I think my heart would stop. It sounds funny: I love my wife. I know my wife is close to me, by me, guiding me. I said this many times before, but I'm sure good has come out of those two evils, the deaths of my wife and son.

Some people ask if I don't feel torn, that I've got a family and that I'm a priest. I feel rather like it's a complementary situation. I feel that I can be a priest to the people I'm supposed to be a priest to: the patients, their families, the staff of this hospital, and those with whom I'm in contact. And I can still be a father and grandfather to my children and grandchildren, by keeping in touch with them, by writing them letters and calling them. I'm still their father, still their grandfather. I pray for them every day, especially at my Mass. So I can help them.

I don't know if I'm any different than if I had become a priest at an earlier age. I think sometimes in the sphere of maybe human sexuality, married life, I might have some experience, but maybe in other fields I have less knowledge or less expertise than some of the priests who have been priests for quite a few years. Particularly in the abuse of alcohol, in the abuse of drugs. I'm learning, I'm trying to grow.

I get lonesome, sure — what do I go home to? Four walls. I get depressed, I get the blues. But I find my way out of them. Sometimes I'm dragging when I leave here at night, mentally and physically, but before I go to bed — this is the truth — I always thank God for all the blessings He's given me: for my good family, for calling me to the priesthood. And the next morning when I say Mass, I always feel something. I feel that sense of gratitude.

I think that you'll find almost any man who's a priest will say, "Why me?" They don't know why. They can't get over it either. God does use the weak of the world. His choices are many times peculiar. I know I don't have all the answers, and I don't claim to have. I know it's not me; it's the Holy Spirit working in me. Say I'm called to an emergency on a Code 4 and I only have time, while I'm running down there, to say, "Holy Spirit, help me," and suddenly I'm in the situation. Most of the time I do and say the right things.

We deal so much with death here. We try to help the grieving relatives. Theoretically, of course, you're not supposed to let yourself become involved that deeply because it would hinder your effectiveness in that situation or in the future. That's what the textbooks say. But practically ... if you're a feeling person, you can't help becoming involved to some degree. You can't really be an effective minister unless you do give part of yourself. I think that a family would sense that you're a phony otherwise. I've had people come to me later and say they knew I was grieving as much as they were. Sometimes, though, I think most of us in this kind of work have a kind of backup device that filters out the real traumatic parts so that we don't get hurt too badly.

Each case is different. There was one a month or so ago ... a woman died and her husband, son, and daughter were there. There was no warmth, no feeling. I guess the daughter was sort of on the outside of the family for something she'd done long ago. Neither her father nor her brother spoke to her, and when they left, they didn't even say good-bye to her. So I went over to her and put my arms around her and kissed her on the forehead. She started to sob and clung to me. They could have given her that support! How do people expect forgiveness from God when they show no mercy? And how can people say they love God when they can't even love each other?

Here at the hospital sometimes we can get attached to patients who've been here a few weeks. You try to help in all aspects of their lives — emotional, psychological, and spiritual. Everybody's got a problem, and a lot of them have more than one. So we have the sacramental aspect of our ministry. We have the Mass — it's televised around the hospital. We have the Sacrament of Reconciliation upon request, and some of them have been away for a long time. After they get to know me, I tell them: "Look, you don't have to worry about going to confession to me. I'm an old beat-up Irishman. I think I'm easy to talk to. I'm not going to holler, downgrade you, or find fault with any damn thing you've ever done, you know." We go face to face, wherever they're comfortable, and they always find it easy.

We lay our hands over the person's head, you know, and I read the words from the book ... because I've never memorized them. I never say the words of absolution — this is the truth: I never say them that I don't get choked up. To think that ... you know ... I'm a priest, I'm helping somebody reconcile with God. It's a tremendous thing. I don't know whether I'll ever get over it. Really! You know, it's a very humbling thing.

I've never said Mass that I don't feel some kind of experience of gratitude that I'm able to say Mass ... that I'm able to say Mass in the context of thanksgiving, praise, and petition. And I try to make each Mass meaningful so that the whole congregation feels they're part of it. And they can see I mean it, so they mean it too.

We all have a mission in life. I guess we have to fulfill our destiny by trying to be open to the Spirit. We are temples of the Holy Spirit and we have to be open, to listen once in a while, to do what God wants us to do. I think many times we don't. I think the Spirit was trying to knock on my door and beat my head in before '73, and I just wouldn't listen.

So I think this change of careers is for the better because, first, I feel that I'm following God's will — God called me, I didn't ask to be a priest; second, I'm able to accomplish some good; and, third, I'm not just existing, I've got a sense of accomplishment, a sense of fulfillment.

In the last year and a half before I entered the seminary, I was enjoying life. I liked going down to Atlantic City. But what was I doing? What was I accomplishing? It wasn't fulfilling. I said to myself: "How many years do I have left? I'd better get on the ball." But my children were good examples to me. My daughters, my sons — each of them doing something. What the hell was the old man doing? Me, I had the time. I talked it over with my boys, particularly one of my sons. I don't know where my family obligations are, really, I said. And they convinced me that my obligations are to myself and to God and to wherever the Spirit leads me.

Like I told somebody: "I'm sixty-six, starting a whole new career. I've got a great future — in back of me!" Aha!

Who knows how long I'll be here — a day? a month? a year? I'm willing to work until God wants to take me home.

JOHN SANDERS

A Musician Finds
His Harmony with God

"I had everything. My dreams had come true. I had been in Duke Ellington's band. I was living a life as a musician. This is what I had trained for, why I had studied at Juilliard. But even with that, I felt it wasn't the end. I wondered where my life was going. And I couldn't help be attracted to the priesthood."

Father John Sanders settles down in the newly redecorated living room of the rectory in Fairfield, Connecticut. He has just come from celebrating the funeral Mass for a seventy-two-year-old man who died of a heart attack. It was a small funeral, with only the immediate family present for Sanders's final prayers.

Holy Family Church, where Sanders is associate pastor, is in a modest, working-class neighborhood of Fairfield; its people, of Polish, Irish, Italian, and Hungarian descent, work in nearby industries or commute to New York. For them, John Sanders is carving out a new career.

As a child in Harlem, Sanders had been nurtured on the Apollo Theater and its big bands. One band in particular, Duke Ellington's, was a compelling magnet, and Sanders dreamed of playing with it one day. When he did, by chance, see his dream fulfilled, Sanders was

overjoyed. The five years of cross-country tours were exciting, re-
warding, and "just wonderful."

Yet there was a growing desire for something more. Priesthood
did not beckon suddenly or dramatically. He had known priests in his
past and continued to make contact with them. Now he hoped to join
with them to do God's work. So he put his trombone away and, at
forty, entered a seminary.

In the warmth of his living room on this winter day, Sanders
flashes a wide smile and remembers his days with Ellington with en-
thusiasm. A shy and modest man, he does not note that in Ellington's
autobiography, Music Is My Mistress, *The Duke called Sanders a*
"brilliant musician" and went .on to say: "I love John Sanders and
think that just about everyone else who knows him loves him for the
great human being that he is." In Fairfield, there is the feeling that a
large number of other people are learning to love John Sanders...

I was attracted to the priesthood, and yet I kept backing
away from it. I felt that I didn't have the education, that maybe I
had waited too long. But my family and my priest-friends helped
me. They said: "Look, the door's not closed. You're not too old."
It just set me off in this direction.

I don't think a vocation is something you reach out and grab.
It's offered to you. It's a gift, really. You think about it, you pray
over it, you talk it over with people because, I think, it works
through people. And then you say, "Well, I accept." Once an invitation is made, it's kind of hard to ignore. You just can't.

I think ever since high school this idea was there, but music
just sort of got in the way and clouded it over for a while. From
what I had read of priesthood and what I had observed of priests,
I just thought this would be a wonderful way to live.

I had models from childhood. I think of coming home from
Mass, or Benediction, or confession and having that wonderful,
exhilarating feeling. And the thought of doing that for others...
"Well," I thought, "that could be a great joy."

When I started out in '65, I was somewhat apprehensive. I
wanted to become a priest, but I was concerned about my years,
and to start again with all this academic training ... well, that was

something. But, as I tell students in the school here: "Don't look at four or five years in the future. Take one year at a time, work with what you're doing now to the best of your ability, and before you know it, it'll be gone." It's like playing one-nighters. You can't play Philadelphia if you're worrying about doing L.A. six weeks later. You've got to go through all these other dates first. Each one has to be in itself a good date.

So now, for me, each day has its own needs and demands, things you have to do. You try to do the best you can and not worry.

You know, I don't think I could have come this far without the support of my family. They've been so wonderful. My family was always very close to the Church, so that became a part of my life. From my mother and dad and my grandparents I got a good foundation. I was an altar boy when I was young, and I sang in the choir whenever I could. When I came home from the Navy, I sang in the choir of the parish church.

Dad was a convert. He was from Sumter, South Carolina, but grew up in New York. My mother's family was primarily West Indian, and she also grew up in New York City. I was born in Elmsford, New York, in 1925, but I was raised in Harlem for the most part. We stayed there until my fourth year of high school. Then we moved to the Bronx and in 1952 we moved to Queens. It's a big family. I'm the oldest, and I have five sisters. Dad worked for the post office all those years, but now he's retired.

My interest in music began in grade school, I think. My parents were very fond of popular and semiclassical music. Dad liked the Victor Herbert-type things. My uncle and aunt liked movies very much, and stage shows, and ... well, I was exposed to that. My aunt used to take me to the Apollo Theater in Harlem, where week after week there was one big band after another. She would take me and my cousin regularly, and then sometimes I would go on my own. The Apollo usually featured a big-name band, a singer, or a group. It could be the Ink Spots one week, Cab Calloway another ... Duke Ellington, Count Basie. They'd have a movie in between.

I fell in love with the big bands. I'd listen to the radio at home — Make Believe Ballroom and those shows. And I'd go to the Apollo, and then later on I'd go downtown to the Paramount Theater and see bands, like Goodman and Dorsey and Glenn Miller.

Of all the bands, Duke Ellington was my favorite. I can never forget sitting in the Apollo Theater and watching this man, this wonderful musician who wrote his music and arranged it for the men in the band. So dignified! All the other bands? You admired them. If you liked jazz, you would enjoy them. But Duke seemed to be so thoughtful, so deep, so unique. Well, I guess the dream started then.

By the time I got to my second year in high school, I was just crazy about these things. So I was able to take trombone lessons and gradually got to be in the high-school band. Music was the biggest part of my life. I was taking a college business course. I was interested in accounting and planning on that as a career. But I knew that music would be an avocation.

I joined the navy just before I turned eighteen in 1943. The draft was inevitable. Well, the high-school band instructor suggested that we make use of our musical ability and possibly play in the navy band. The navy looked good. It seemed to be in a special class and to offer many opportunities. I joined the navy and did end up in the navy band.

I served primarily in San Diego on a section base, and early in '46 we were sent up to Treasure Island in the San Francisco Bay area. It was a time when people were being discharged, and we had to kind of sit it out there. In San Diego we had specific duties, a full schedule during the day, and we played for dances, shows, military ceremonies — things like that. I was discharged in May of '46.

By the time I got out of the navy, I could see music as a career. But in the navy I had become close to a chaplain, Father Joseph Fulton, up in the Oakland area, and he encouraged me to go into the seminary. But I couldn't see anything else but music. I knew that I wanted to go to music school. At that time I just couldn't see the religious life. Oh, I had thought of it, off and on, in grade school and high school. Wherever I went, I admired the priests, looked upon them as rather special. But I thought of it only in a rather distant way.

When I got out of the navy, I decided to go to The Juilliard School of Music. I didn't see going back to accounting or any other field. I was accepted there and did a four-year diploma course in three years. I was in the orchestral instruments department. I studied the trombone and took the related music subjects, such as theory, harmony, piano. It was quite a life, bumping into people every day who were all going into music. It was exciting just being there. At this time we were living in the Bronx, and I was riding the subway back and forth because Juilliard at that time was near Riverside Drive and 122nd Street.

Music became such a big part of my life, and I wanted to become an all-round musician. I liked jazz, but I didn't want to train for that alone. I was playing in dance orchestras on weekends. I wanted to be prepared for everything — I liked it all. I guess I even thought of symphony orchestras. And somewhere in the back of my mind I thought, "Wouldn't it be something to play with a big band — Basie, Lunceford, Ellington!" But Ellington was special.

Well, I made friends with a trombone player with the band, Lawrence Brown. He was the first one I actually had the nerve to go up and meet, and he was encouraging. When I got out of Juilliard in 1949, like most musicians in New York, I began to job around ... club dates, different groups. And as you played with different groups, musicians would recommend you to other groups, and before you knew it, you were getting more steady work. I finally got steady work by way of the Savoy Ballroom in Harlem. This is where people went to dance to all the big bands. The bands from downtown would come uptown and there would be music battles — Chick Webb, Fletcher Henderson, or someone like Louie Armstrong might battle Benny Goodman or Tommy Dorsey. And the winner? Well, I don't think anyone really knew or cared.

When I was working at the Savoy, I was playing with a new group under Lucky Thompson, and while I was there, I got to know Mercer Ellington, Duke's son. Well, when Duke needed a

43

trombone player for a cross-country tour in 1953, Mercer suggested I go to Duke. It seems that Juan Tizol, who had been playing trombone for Duke for many years, wanted to return to his home in California and take care of some business, and Duke needed a replacement. Mercer said I should go and see Duke, just say that he sent me. This was the way they did it — if Mercer sent you, that was enough for Duke. Well, I went backstage. Duke was at the Apollo Theater then, playing a date with Pearl Bailey. The name John Sanders didn't mean anything, but he did know Lucky Thompson. So he suggested that I sit in with the band that night. It was a Thursday and they were closing. So I hurried back to Queens, got my trombone, and came back in time for the next show — I took the A train as a matter of fact. Juan Tizol gave me his jacket, showed me the music, and said, "You'll be okay." Well, by no means do I consider myself a crack musician, but I got by. I had followed the band and I knew the music, so I could pick up the pieces. After the show, Duke said, "Why don't you come out on tour a few days." He made no commitment.

So we started one-nighting it — to Virginia, North Carolina, and then to the South and West. A few days went by and Duke never said anything. We ended up in San Diego, and Tizol showed up. This is six weeks later. Well, they gave me a railroad ticket back home, but they said: "Well, John, maybe you'll be back with us someday. You never know."

I resumed my work with Lucky Thompson at the Savoy Ballroom, but in February '54, Duke himself called me on the phone one night. He said: "Can you come back with the band? Juan is going to stay in California." The chair was empty. I said yes, immediately.

It was a dream come true. That's the only way I can express it. The fact that I had gone out with the band for a few weeks was wonderful. That was enough to set me up for life. But to have him call me back and say, "Can you join the band?"... well, that was beyond my fondest hopes. So I began playing with Duke in Toronto in February 1954, and I stayed with the band till September of 1959. Five years. Just wonderful.

Duke was such a warm person, thoughtful, very considerate

of other people. He made you feel you had something to offer. He knew you were around. You weren't just a guy in the band. You worked hard because Duke worked hard. But the guys admired Duke; he allowed them to be themselves. They didn't lose their identity by being in the band because Duke's band was so unique. The band at that time was about fifteen members: seven or eight brass, five reeds, and three or four rhythms.

When I was in the band ... let's see ... there were wonderful musicians, like Harry Carney, Johnny Hodges, and Ray Nance — men who had been with Duke for many many years. What a joy to work with them, to hear them night after night! And, of course, how can I ever forget those two fine trombonists, Britt Woodman and Quentin "Butter" Jackson, who helped me settle down in Juan Tizol's chair. You can never take someone's place — you simply try hard to carry on a tradition. I'll always be grateful to Lawrence, Juan, Britt, and Butter.

Duke wrote for the men. His whole life was writing new music for the men to play. For a concert, he'd write something to be performed by the orchestra, like a suite, but he also would write things to showcase the ability of individual orchestra members.

He drew out the best in you. He only called a rehearsal on pieces that were long, that had to be put together. But the men were such wonderful musicians. They were so sensitive to his writing, they could feel it instantly.

We did a lot of recordings in the fifties, on Columbia primarily. I don't play them that often anymore, but I do have them. Once in a while I put them on and, you know, I can't believe what a wonderful experience that was.

Duke was a very religious man. He never talked religion, but he had this tremendous religious feeling about him, a reverence and respect for God. When he started writing sacred concerts, that was to him the greatest privilege. He couldn't make it to my ordination, but he came to my first Mass. He had just come in from a date and somehow ended up in St. Pius Church. At the reception afterwards, people asked him for his autograph, but he declined. He said, "I'm sorry. This is John's day."

In February '74 he came to the Shakespeare Theater in Stratford. At that time I was at Blessed Sacrament Church — my first assignment — in nearby Bridgeport, and a group of us from the parish attended the concert. Duke played a special thing for me that night. Backstage was jammed, but we managed to get to Duke's dressing room, where I happily introduced a priest, several nuns and parishioners. How patient and kind he was that evening after a long and tiring concert. You see, Duke had been ailing and under a doctor's care. He had mentioned to me that previous December in New York that he wasn't sure of making the Shakespeare date. Duke passed away in May 1974, in New York City. I wish I had been closer to him in those last years.

Traveling? Well, it was exciting, yes, but terribly hard at times. For me it was an education doing the one-nighters, playing big towns and little towns, traveling north and south, east and west throughout the United States and Canada. It was a tremendous experience. The older men could take it. They'd been through it so many times, so many years.

We came back to New York from time to time, for two or three weeks at a time. We might play Birdland down on Broadway, or another nightclub, like Basin Street, or a week at the Apollo Theater. However, it was a time to be with the family again. In Chicago or LA, the band could sit down in one place for two or three weeks at a time too.

I couldn't sleep on the bus too much. I was always up at night. I just wasn't one of these people who could sit on a bus and completely relax. I think that was the hardest part for me, the time at night. You'd miss home. You'd pass the towns, and you'd just long to be in a home. If you could sleep through it, it was better.

While I was with the band on the road, I met Father Norman O'Connor. He's a Paulist priest, and in '54 he was stationed up in Boston. He was a very close admirer of Ellington and followed jazz. In fact, he was the master of ceremonies at the Newport Jazz Festival in 1956. Well, we became close friends. Also around that time — I think it was in '56 — I was in Salt Lake City, and I met another priest, Father William McDougal, and I started talking to him about vocations, what was going to happen to my life. He suggested that I get in touch with the Catholic Center in Ottawa. They gave a course, a correspondence course, about a person's state of life. So I got in touch with them, and they began to send me material. Wonderful material. I hadn't thought about all of this because I was so busy. I really hadn't thought of anything else beyond the band.

Well, I read the vocational material on the bus and in the hotel. I remember going out to a quiet spot on the Oak Street beach in Chicago one day with the material. The one thing that fascinated me in this course was the section on the priesthood. By 1959 I knew I had to get back to New York. I missed my family, and I really wanted to get back home. But also after taking this course, I needed to go home and settle down and see where my life was heading. I knew that even though my dream of joining the Ellington band was fulfilled, it wasn't the end. The priesthood? Well, I thought it was kind of late because I hadn't gone to college and I was in my early thirties. My understanding was that one started in high school to prepare for the priesthood.

Well, back in New York, I got to know a young priest, Father Thomas Hicks, at my parish in Jamaica, Queens. And I was able to resume my friendship with Father O'Connor, who had been transferred to New York. Both of them were so instrumental, so helpful to me in seeing the possibility of a vocation to the priesthood. I wasn't too old; it wasn't too late. There were special places of study for the late vocation. Father O'Connor encouraged me to take an evening course in philosophy at Fordham University. Perhaps it would allow me the chance to get the feel of a classroom again. And then there were those wonderful evenings spent with Father Hicks in a small Bible group at St. Pius.

When I left the band, I kept my hand in music. The first year I worked on a research project for a small group of Ellington friends: his doctor; his arranger, Billy Strayhorn; and an executive for Columbia Records. They wanted me to collect all of Duke's manuscripts and put them in order. They said it was a shame to have them all over the place — his house, his publishing office, his son's house, Billy Strayhorn's house. So they asked me, before I could unpack almost, if I could work on this. You see, I did a lot of copying of Duke's music, as Juan Tizol had done. I was familiar with his handwriting. So it was up to me to go through the closets and drawers and trunks of music. I'd put it together. I'd go to publishers and ask for old lead sheets. Sometimes I'd put it together from orchestral parts and, from the parts, make a score. Sometimes I'd have to listen to old recordings and try to get the melody down. One day in 1960 a truck came and picked it all up. It was originally planned to present this to Duke at some affair, but they couldn't get Duke to do it. He'd have no part of it. It would seem like that would mean that he was retiring, that he wasn't writing any more. So it ended up in a storehouse.

After that I worked at Schirmer's Music Store, and then at Juilliard as an orchestra librarian, where I stayed until I went to the seminary in 1965. Still, being an old trombone player, I played occasionally. Primarily, I ended up in the Queens Symphony Orchestra. They gave some nice concerts, and I enjoyed that. I made the symphony ... finally.

In 1965 I had gone on a retreat to a Trappist monastery with Father Hicks, and after some good long talks with Father O'Connor and Father Hicks, I finally made a decision to go into the seminary. Oh yes, I was still concerned about several things — my age ... my education. I had done all right in high school and at Juilliard. What about going back to college at forty? But starting all over again was part of accepting the call — the invitation to be a part of the priesthood of Jesus Christ. It all seemed clearer now, more hopeful.

And I really did want to become a priest. You know, you'd see Our Lord in priests, and you'd say: "I'd like to be a part of this. I'd like to do His work, celebrate Mass, bring sacraments, help people." It seems like you are working out your own salvation and, hopefully, that you are helping others toward it too.

But I don't think I could have done it without the encouragement of the priests and my family. My family was very happy for me. My mother and dad never pushed me toward the seminary though. They showed me newspaper stories of men who had done it later in life; but they knew it had to come from me.

Then there were eight years of study, first at Holy Apostles in Cromwell, Connecticut, and then at Pope John XXIII in Weston, Massachusetts. Then I was ordained at Blessed Sacrament Church in Bridgeport, Connecticut. I stayed there until 1975, when I came here to Holy Family.

I think I can say that I enjoy everything I do as a priest. It's all so different. Some things are harder than others. I enjoy celebrating Mass. Preaching is a challenge, but I find I enjoy doing it if I can help people see where the Gospels and the word of God apply to their lives. I enjoy visiting the sick. I enjoy the young people in school — their ideals, their views, their innocence. I find that very refreshing.

The thing I find most difficult is dealing with a complicated marriage situation. When you try to straighten out these matters — especially when you're dealing with people who don't understand the laws of the Church or who haven't lived their faith, and they want you to untangle the situation — well, I find that the stickiest part of it because there are laws that we have to follow.

I find it ever challenging, always. Whatever you did last week or last month, while it has its good effects, you have to keep thinking and addressing yourself to the new situation. Every weekend is not just a weekend of Masses, but a whole new situation. While Lent, Advent, and the other seasons come and go, they're different, and you have to keep sharpening up for them and seeing how you are going to make this effective and help people.

Part of it is that you have to read a lot, and the one thing that does concern me is not having the time to read as much as I'd like. I wish I had more time, and I have to keep working on that. You can't give what you don't have. Just like a musician, you know. If you don't practice, you can't give or perform. You may want to do it, and you might have the ability to do it; but if you don't work at it, it's not going to be there when you need it.

The thing that keeps you going is that your priesthood is affirmed by the people. You don't always see it in the concrete. In certain fields or professions, one can measure his work, see his accomplishments. In the priesthood, it's not always that definable

... the things you do from day to day, week to week. Sometimes you think you're just going and going. One minute you're teaching or visiting the sick, and then you're helping young people get ready for marriage ... being with a family at a baptism ... or a wake. You're in touch with people in so many different important moments in their lives. You become a part of that. Sometimes it may be more touch and go; other times it's more ongoing, but it's there and they are thankful for it. If you ever get a little bit winded, you think of these things that affirm your priesthood. They may not say it, but you sense it; and it's a wonderful thing.

I know people must wonder about it at times. Here I am, the only black priest in the whole diocese. At Blessed Sacrament we were in a predominantly black neighborhood; here's it's mostly white. But I don't think about it. All my life I've been associated with all people. Even when we lived in Harlem, I was always going out beyond. I never stayed in Harlem. My family always lived in mixed neighborhoods. In fact, many times they lived in predominantly white neighborhoods.

There are times when it does help. If black people don't know who else to approach, they can always call on me. And I'm director of the Black Apostolate for the diocese. Right now we're having a little collection to help black students going to Catholic schools, kids who want a Catholic education but can't afford it.

But here in the parish ... well, I just see this as a parish of people. I never think in terms of what they are and what I am. I've never seen myself as a black priest; I'm a priest who happens to be black.

Sometimes, when people know my background, they ask me to give a little talk — and bring my trombone. So I practice. Right now I'm rusty. Haven't played for months. I tell them about my life, and I play some old Ellington songs. Maybe I've missed the boat on this, but every year I say I'm going to play something in church for Christmas or Easter, and I haven't done it. I find that if I'm not up on it, I can't begin to think about playing.

I think music will always be a part of my life. I enjoy listening to concerts, something special on television, records. I never bought records before in my life; now I'll pick something up. It could be a symphony that I like, or — like the other day — a Schubert quintet that I heard at Juilliard but never owned before. And I enjoy buying some of the old Ellington things.

I've never thought about what would have happened if I had become a priest earlier. I just think my life had taken a certain course and it had to come when it did. Coming late in life, I'm grateful for it, grateful for the years I have left as a priest. I feel I have to be more conscious of that because it has come to me late in life. Someone at the seminary said that if you have even one year as a priest, you've been given a lot. I've often thought about that.

JAMES MAYO

A Young Widower at Peace

"I'm not as driven. I think that's part of the peace. God is active in my life now. He and I are working as a team; it's not me working against Him. I think that's what was driving me. I was running ... inside I was running. If I could keep busy enough in social-type work, then I wouldn't have to worry about God saying 'Come on, I want you.' I didn't realize I had a call. I didn't know what I was doing.

"When I decided that this was what I wanted to do the rest of my life, a peace, an inner peace, just came over me. People who know me at home will say: 'You're just so peaceful. You just glow, you radiate all over the place.' I was a pretty happy man before, but this is even more."

James Mayo ticks off the list of his community service efforts. It sounds as though there weren't many other people to do the work in Nantucket, Massachusetts.

Mayo's previous involvements include volunteer work as: scout-master, Explorer adviser, camp ranger and camp director for the Boy Scouts of America; member of the board of directors of Nantucket Columbus Associates, Inc.; president and secretary of the Nantucket

Firemen's Association; secretary of the Massachusetts Society for the Prevention of Cruelty to Children; director of the Nantucket Chamber of Commerce; leader in the Red Cross bloodmobile program and the Council on Alcoholism; tail twister for the Lions Club; forest warden; assistant civil defense director; member of the Nantucket Planning Board; grand knight of the Knights of Columbus; secretary-treasurer of the St. Vincent de Paul Society; chairman of the Catholic Charities Appeal.

A big, strapping man – six feet, two hundred pounds – Mayo has enormous energy. He may also be a classic case of a workaholic. Besides all those civic involvements, he held down two jobs for a number of years, one of them as a Nantucket policeman.

Mayo got involved because he wanted to, and somehow he found the time. But he admits now that there was more to it. Like many of us, he did some things for the sake of the challenge and to be what he calls "affirmed." In other words, he liked the praise he got for doing a job well.

It is easy to imagine Mayo doing this for the rest of his life, earning countless honors and certificates and, on his retirement, testimonial dinners. If a heart attack wouldn't have killed him off first, of course. The civic drive was diminished briefly when he was married, but the marriage ended tragically sixteen months later, when his wife died in childbirth. Then he became even more compulsive – until he realized that God was calling him to the priesthood.

Mayo believes that each of the events of his life had a purpose, that even his marriage was a way of guiding him to the priesthood. His life, he says, has not been a series of turns but a growing process. He says he is not starting out fresh but is continuing to grow. "The experiences of the past are a part of me, and all I can do is make them more valuable."

At forty-three he was ordained. At his first parish, Sacred Heart, in Warner Robins, Georgia, his Massachusetts accent mingles with the "y'alls" of his new parishioners...

I still have a drive, sure. I hope I never lose that. But it's a different kind of drive now. I have that peace, that inner peace.

In the past, I think it was important that I would be the

leader. I don't need that now. I have a lot of weaknesses, but that's okay. I can live with them. I don't have to be number one. And every time I swing the bat, I don't have to go for the fence. Before, I had to have a home run every time I got to bat. Everybody cheers somebody who hits a home run. I don't need that type of affirmation anymore. I know who I am now. And I can be honest with myself. It's okay for me to screw up. It's a neat feeling, in fact, to say, "Well, Mayo, you blew that one."

For example, when we built a new shower house at Boy Scout camp, probably a six-month project, it was a case of go, go, go to get it ready. When it was done, it was a real letdown, and I immediately started looking for something new to do. Now after I do something, there's no letdown. The inner peace is a gentleness... It's kind of hard to explain. You know something is over, but you don't have to look around for the next job. You know there's going to be one. And you come down off the high ready to go on to what's ahead of you. It's a nice peace. You don't have to look for things to build up your ego.

I was born in Nantucket and grew up there. You know, five thousand people in the wintertime and about fifty thousand in the summer. We had wall-to-wall people. I was the baby of the family. I have a brother and a sister and through school all I ever heard was how brilliant my brother and sister were. So Jim Mayo decided he'd be different and just have a good time and never worry about marks.

My dad died of pneumonia the year I was born, so my mum raised us. When we were small, she took in laundry; as we got older, she was a waitress in a local guesthouse. As I got into high school, she opened and closed houses on the island. I worked in a drugstore as a stock boy, and I had my own lawn business. I even had a couple of kids working for me.

After high school I went into the service, the Air Force, and was stationed in Germany. That was in 1954. I took some off-campus courses from the University of Maryland while I was in the service, and I started to realize that an education was kind of valuable. I also woke up to the fact that I had as much brains as my brother and sister did, and I started to use them.

When I came back, I started to work for the steamship authority that runs into the island. Then I went to work for an insurance company. I went to insurance school in Baltimore. I was selling insurance and also doing some claims investigations. That lasted ... three and a half, four years.

I have an aggressive-type personality. I just like to do things, like to be on the go. People have a tendency to like me, and I like people. The guy that I worked for was not overly pleased with this, and he and I were coming to misunderstandings. People would come in and ask for me rather than for him. So I left there and went to work as a dairy manager in a chain store. And I enjoyed that — until again I ran into problems. You're a number, you're not a person. And they're great for planagrams. I was selling a lot of yogurt and the planagram called for like two feet of yogurt and I had eight feet of yogurt. But it was selling, so I figured it was justified. Well, every time the bosses would come down to the store, I'd catch hell for that. One day I left there and walked across the street to a hardware store and was hired as a sporting goods manager. They'd been after me for a while.

All the time, I was doing these other jobs. The year I came back from the service they needed a cop in Sconsot, for the movie theater and for the village patrol. So I hired on and sort of enjoyed police work, found it interesting. And then I went to work full time with the Nantucket Police Department. I worked a regular shift ... worked out with the other job I was on. Every now and then I'd hit a midnight to eight and have to go from there to the other job.

I think I was a good cop: fair, just — but frustrated most of the time. Because of the tension that's there, I think.

I remember taking a kid home one night, probably sixteen or seventeen, completely smashed right out of it. I brought him home rather than bring him in and book him. In a small town a lot of little things like that are done. I saw his father the next day and told him I had brought his son home and that the boy was completely smacko. He said, "Not my son. My son doesn't drink." Which is a typical parent reaction. That's frustrating as hell. I did pick the kid up again, only this time I took him to the station and called his father and said I had somebody who claimed to be his son but I was sure it wasn't because this kid was stiff and his boy didn't drink. And his father came down and bailed him out.

I think it's things like that that eventually start speaking to you. A cop is not always hard-nosed. You know the expression, "He'd book his mother." Well, I've worked with guys like that, but the majority are very, very decent. It was incidents like that, though, that made me see I really wasn't cut out to be a cop. I didn't like going to court. You arrest somebody for a traffic violation or whatever and you're doing your job. But then you see the guy losing his license and maybe his job because maybe his job depends on his having a license. Well, maybe the fella needed guidance, maybe he had problems at home, maybe a lot of other things.

I guess the one time I really thought I was doomed was a marital dispute. I went in the back door of the house. You always leave the door open so you can get out, but this door had a pump hinge on it, and as the husband came charging out from the living room with a twelve-gauge shotgun, I backed into the door and closed it. And I couldn't get out. There I was with this shotgun shoved into my gut. And there was no way my partner could have come in to do something for me. It took me about an hour to talk him through the shells in that gun. He wouldn't hand me the gun. He'd just pump them through, one at a time. And yet, while this whole thing was going on, I didn't feel any real scared feeling. But when it was all over, I went back to the station and —I don't mind telling you—I did have to change my shorts.

I never fired at anybody. The closest I came was the night an alarm went off in a shop. My partner took the front door and I took the back door. I could see a person inside, so I drew my revolver and jammed it in his ribs and told him to reach or I'd blast him. He tried to tell me he was the owner and had set his own alarm off. Well, turned out he *was* the owner! He told me the next day his ribs were rather sore and black and blue.

After I came back from the service, I started going with Eileen. I had gone with her off and on during high school. We kind of broke up and then went back together again. Then we became very serious and, finally, in June of '62, we got married. I was in the insurance business at that time.

After a year and a half of marriage, Eileen died in childbirth. She only had one kidney; we didn't know that. She had uremia and went into a coma and that's where she stayed. She was twenty-four; I was twenty-six.

I think our marriage was pretty good. We got along well, prayed a lot together, went to Mass together. And we talked a lot before our marriage about what marriage is — is it a contract? a license to sleep together? And we agreed that if God wasn't involved in it, then it wasn't a marriage. And that... like Christ became one with His Church. Well, marriage is the same thing — two people sharing and working toward becoming one.

I think she was probably a little ahead of me in her relationship to God. She had gone to a parochial school for one thing; I hadn't. But we agreed pretty much on the basics. I think she helped me with my prayer because she was a prayerful person.

I don't want you to get the idea that we prayed all the time, but to say grace at the table was very common, and, after liturgy, to say, "Now, how can we apply that to our lives?" God was active in our lives. Eileen had a very strong devotion to Mary, and that kind of helped me.

I guess our plans for the future may have been idealistic. We looked forward to either buying the place we were living in — it was a house with three cottages with it — or getting a piece of land out of town and building out there. I can remember we had a heated discussion because of the distance the kids would have to travel.

I don't remember if we ever came up with a number on how many kids we'd have. I do know she wanted a girl and I wanted a boy. And we had agreed that if we couldn't have any children, we would adopt.

When she came in the insurance office and told me she was pregnant, I flew around the office with joy. We had no indication of her illness beforehand. She was kind of a frail girl. A little, petite person. When you're in love, you're blind anyway.

Yeah, I was devastated by my wife's death. I couldn't handle it. I was not just mad at God, I was totally angry at God, just as angry as I could possibly get. I left the Church. I had nothing to do with Him. I didn't want to dialogue with Him, I didn't want to talk with Him. I thought God and I had a good relationship before that, at least what I thought was a good relationship. Now I know it was not. I think it was sort of an adolescent kind of relationship, a bargaining type. You give me what I want, God, and I'll do this for you. You know — if you don't do this, God's gonna getcha.

I say I left the Church, but that's not really true. I still went to Mass and went through the motions because of my mum, not wanting to crush her. She really couldn't appreciate what I was going through: the hurt, the pain, and the anger — and blaming God for it. So there was still a little bit of a thread there.

About two years later, I was in a nursing home taking absentee ballots, and there was a girl there who was a complete vegetable. If Eileen had lived, she would have been like that. The girl's husband came in and brought her a beautiful bouquet of flowers, and I watched this whole transaction take place. Her eyes didn't even blink or warm or light up. It was like a carrot sitting there. Nothing. I guess I turned as white as a ghost and started to sweat. The head nurse, who was with me, asked what happened to me in there. "You're not the same person that went in that room," she said. "You're completely different. This is the first time I've seen your eyes glow and sparkle. All of a sudden you're radiating. You haven't looked like that in years." I said, "I just realized that God loves me ... how good God really was to me."

It could have been Eileen sitting there. I didn't know how that man went through it. The pain and the hurt that I had was really nothing compared to what he had. And from that point forward everything in my life just turned around. That was the first time, I think, that I really felt the presence of God in my life.

He knew what He was doing. Through my whole life, I can see the things that have led me to where I am now. But there wasn't, at that point, any thought of becoming a priest.

I went back to church with much more vigor, wanting to

know about God, about my own faith. I started reading — getting into theology, the lives of the saints, commentaries on the Gospels, *The Imitation of Christ*, Merton, books by John Powell. And I started teaching CCD. And I became a lector in the church and took over the altar boy training.

I got even more active in other things. Yes, I was a civic nut. I had been active in the Boy Scouts ever since I was in the service. These kids really needed something. When I grew up on the island, we made up our own activities. I really hated to see kids hanging around becoming drugstore cowboys. A good Scout program held their interest.

Yeah, I wish I had a son. I won't deny that. My child was a boy. He would have been named Kevin. I enjoy working with youth, even today. They have so much to offer, and I think they are so misunderstood. They want things explained to them. I came up out of a generation that said, "Hey, you do it," and that's it.

So I got more involved in Scouts. I was a scoutmaster, a camp director, and I had an Explorer post. They started a new cablevision operation on the island, and I wound up doing my own TV series, *Cavalcade of Scouting*. After the nursing home incident, it was very difficult for me to say no when somebody asked me to do something.

And I dated all the time. Nobody in particular, a lot in general. I seriously thought about getting married again. And yet there was still something there with Eileen. I found it very difficult to get over that barrier. I was going with the wife of a buddy of mine who had died. They had a couple of kids, and I was very close to their kids. I had promised him that I would watch over them. We went together for about four years, off and on, and we'd both say the same thing — I reminded her of things that he did, and she reminded me of things that Eileen did.

More and more, I came to the realization that God was calling me. But I kept avoiding it. Well, in February of '74 I was on a speaking tour for the Boy Scouts, and I couldn't get home because of a snowstorm. I had to spend the night in a motel. I was very relaxed; it had been a good tour and things had gone well. I woke up at three o'clock in the morning — I had glanced at the clock — and this voice said, "James, I want you." It was just that loud, just that clear, and I sat right smack up in bed. But I thought nothing of it and lay down and went right back to sleep. The next morning on the plane home, I was reading Merton's *Seeds of Contemplation* and I looked out. It was just so beautiful, the way it usually is after a storm. White puffy clouds — oh, it was just neat! And the whole thing that happened the night before came back to me. But I knew I didn't want to answer the call.

My life became very mixed up after that. An awful lot of tensions inside of me. I was no longer comfortable with anything that I did. I played a lot of golf that summer. Just beat the hell out of that golf ball. The guys who played with me no longer wanted to. My disposition was just nasty. I was not happy, had no inner peace at all: I was miserable.

That fall I took a week's vacation at Pinehurst, North Carolina. I took my golf clubs and a book by Thomas Merton. One day, during the week, I was playing with these guys I'd picked up on the tee. All of a sudden, I was on the tee and I was working through my problems, and I said, "Yeah, Lord, get off my back. I'm coming." And I came through with the club, and all I can remember is the guys saying, "Wow! What got into you?" I drove the ball 250 yards, just as clear and straight. I never had a better drive in my life. "Just made the biggest decision of my life," I said. And all of a sudden, all this tension, this anger, just sort of disappeared.

On Saturday, I came home and told my mother. That Sunday I was doing the readings at church. The second reading was from Luke, and I almost broke down. It said, "Come, follow me."

So the decision was made. I gave away my shotguns, my rifles, my fishing gear, my model trains. The first time I tried to do it, I couldn't. I could have put them in storage, but I thought the fact of not having those things was important. I kept my golf clubs. I didn't sell my house. My mum lives in it, so I still own the house. Me and the bank, that is.

It was kind of hard to adjust to seminary life at first — going to meals on time, getting to class, studying, using the same shower, the same john with a bunch of other guys. But you get used to it. I have no formal college, so I took a college equivalency test, and I really proved myself. I had a three point seven average the last couple of semesters — this was at Sacred Heart School of Theology, outside Milwaukee.

Lately I've been reading a lot of Carl Jung, who talks about how God spoke to the prophets in dreams and visions. It think He still speaks to us today in dreams and visions. I think that's what that was that night I heard that voice. And I see other signs too — a rainbow often appears at a crisis point in my life. I know some people may criticize me and say that the "signs" I see are just coincidences, the answers I have are too pat. But that's their problem. I feel for them. That's me, and I'm comfortable with it. If it was just the signs, yeah. But it's more than that. God is as active in people's lives today as when He was leading the people through the desert. He's no different. If He could speak through the prophets, to Moses — to those people — He can speak to us in the same way.

I think one of the reasons I have this personal relationship with the Lord is that I can talk to Christ just like I talk to anyone else. The only times I manage to get myself into a pickle are when I don't consult Him — or when I don't listen to Him. The Lord and I do things together. Maybe I don't always appreciate what He wants me to do, but I know He's there.

I think there is a renewal in my life, but I don't like to use the term "born again," only because the fundamentalists use it, and they use it in the wrong context. My faith is in my Lord and my Savior, Christ. You know this'll sound like heresy, but even if you could prove to me that Christ wasn't born of the Virgin, that would make no difference. How He got here has nothing to do with my faith. My faith is in Christ: that He walked and talked and breathed, that He was crucified, and that He was resurrected.

Pastoral life is much better than I ever expected it to be. It's frustrating at times, but very rewarding. I find that when I'm counseling people, I'm ministering to them; but in some ways they're ministering to me too. Before, I always seemed to have the answers. I think I've learned, finally, that I don't. The activity of God in me is much more than it ever was, and I see it much more in people. When you see a person come and say that his life is in shambles and he wants to put it back together again, to me that's a great moment in that person's life. To me, that's rewarding. When I'm administering Baptism, it's awesome to see the new life that the parents have. And I'm renewed myself.

To me, a priest is a cultic leader. A priest has to be a man of prayer, and I don't mean just private prayer. Someone who is able to lead in prayer, being a prayerful man himself. A person who is open to the Spirit, able to see the activity of God in his life and to share that with other people. His mission is giving strength to other people, helping them have feelings, being an agent for Christ. As I see it, a priest is compassionate, gentle, kind — and an SOB when necessary. He needs to be honest with people, needs to take people where they're at and help them to grow; to minister the sacraments so they can get closer to God.

You see, I'm Jim Mayo, who happens to be a priest; I'm not priest-Jim Mayo. I think that humanness is what's important. When I celebrate liturgy, I hope I become transparent so that the real significance of Christ comes through ... that people can pray as a community, that they don't see a bunch of gaudy vestments, but that the liturgy becomes a prayer.

I think the whole mentality of priesthood is changing. The priest was always up on the pedestal, better than everybody else. Now we're starting to say the priest is called by his people to be their leader, to share with them. He's human, like Christ was human, and it's okay for a priest to cry, to tell people he's lonely, to share with people his burdens, to wear civilian clothes, to like to bowl, to like to dance — things that humans do. A priest does not just celebrate liturgy and dispense the sacraments and go home to his rectory and lock himself in his room and listen to the radio and drink a bottle of scotch. That's what forces him to drink the scotch! "See, I can't talk to father because he's got a collar on." "Father never swears." That sort of thing. Come on. It's not real. A priest has his wants and he's just as sinful as the next person. That's difficult for people to accept. I'm sure that people in my parish have eighty times more faith than I've got.

I don't think that young people just out of high school should go into the seminary. They need a little bit of experience under their belts. I think I am more qualified because of my experience, my background, the maturing of me as a person, the ups and downs I've had with my own religious experiences, my encounters with Christ.

When somebody loses somebody in their family, I can share that. I can feel that hurt, the pain. I know what they're going through. I can say it's okay to cry, it's okay to "hate" God right now. If somebody had been able to do that with me when I lost Eileen, I wouldn't have had the problems with the Church that I had. The priest, who happened to be a very young guy, couldn't handle it any more than I could; but I think if he had been in the world a little bit, maybe he could have sat down with me and said," It's okay to 'hate' God right now, Jim. It's okay to be angry." Instead of saying, "Well, you know, if you were God and went to a flower garden, you'd pick the most beautiful flower." Well, that reeks to me. I can't stand that. That's not an answer: that's nothing. It's not even holy and pious. It's crap. And that sort of thing can turn people right off at a very crucial point in their life.

I'm not saying that we're smarter, that we have any more answers or are any more pastoral, but I think we have maturity on our side. A kid, unless he had some hell of a rough life, would find that difficult.

I think it's difficult for a kid eighteen, nineteen years old, a guy who has not experienced himself, his own humanity, to know what to do when he's close to a woman. What goes on inside of him? I think a lot of guys who enter the priesthood early deny that anything happens, and later they find they have problems. Maybe that's why they turn to alcohol. Because it's okay to say, "Yeah, that's a neat-looking chick." You're not denying the fact, you recognize it. God made it; it's beautiful.

What about women? Is that a problem? Yeah, it's a problem. I'm human. It's just where you want to put your values, what you want to do, where you're at. I think anybody who denies that is denying his humanity. If you look at celibacy as a no-sex clause in the priesthood, then you're going to have problems. But if you look at celibacy as the giving of yourself to the whole community, being able to share yourself with all those people, being able to love all of them and let all of them love you, then celibacy shouldn't be anything you can't live with. If you isolate yourself and say you can't look at women because you're celibate, then you're going to have problems.

Do I feel married today? Yes, but in a different sense. There's a huge family out there, and as long as I allow them to minister to me as much as I minister to them, then that's family. But if I become the big daddy who has all the answers—well, horseshit.

My marriage is part of my past, a part of my present, a part of my future. Do I see Eileen here, there, and everywhere? No. But the fact is that I know I was married. I know that I had a good relationship with Eileen, that we enjoyed life and planned for the future. And I think that's partly where I'm at today. I think that's part of what I had to go through before I answered the call. I pray to her because I believe we can pray to the dead for intercession. I'm sure there are times that things have happened to me that she's responsible for. And I believe I'll be united with Eileen someday. I don't believe there are marriages in heaven, but I do believe that people are united.

I think about the past. There are a lot of times I think, "Yeah, I wish I had done this twenty years ago." But that's unreal. The fact is that twenty years ago I couldn't have done this. I had to go through all those things — the pain, the loss, the maturing. I'm different. I've grown. And if I had started twenty years ago, I wouldn't be at this point now.

And if I had to go back and do this all over again ... yes, I'd do it all over again. This way.

GEORGE NICHOLSON

A New Man in a New Church

"If Vatican II hadn't happened, I would never have been a priest. Because I believe — and this is my own personal opinion — that the Church that I knew prior to the Second Vatican Council and in which I grew up was a dying institution. It would have gone off the face of the earth. It was irrelevant."

St. Joan of Arc Parish stretches over twenty square blocks in the Jackson Heights section of Queens, New York. Numerous high-rise apartment buildings, which once housed mainly Irish, Italians, and Polish, are now providing homes for the newly arrived Colombians, Cubans, and Argentines. A walk down any street provides a glimpse of a dramatic ethnic mix.

In the red brick rectory at Eighty-second Street and Thirty-fifth Avenue, Father George Nicholson, thirty-nine, talks about the contrasts in his life: the teeming world at his doorstep, compared with the small town in upstate New York where he was born; the Catholic Church of the post-Vatican II era, compared with the one he grew up in; even the changes in his personality, outlook, and concerns that have transformed what he calls "an upstate Republican conservative" into a priest who looks to the needs of his people.

Many of the changes were gradual, but Nicholson says it was the voice of God, heard at a funeral Mass, that called him directly to the priesthood.

When Nicholson talks about the opportunities and challenges facing the Church now, he sits on the edge of his chair and gets excited...

Now ... now, I believe the Church faces the challenge of the ages. It stands with the possibility of bringing all people together in the Body of Christ. It stands as a beacon and a light. Naturally, it is fraught with human frustration and the burdens of all kinds of things, but I think now it is a Church with vision, a Church that can proclaim the Gospel in a new way.

Sure, a lot of people say it is still irrelevant, but that's because they don't understand the Church. They don't know what it is today: that I am the Church, that the people are the Church, that God is calling us — as Isaiah says in this Sunday's reading — to be a people who give Him praise.

For me, this is all so exciting. During the time I had cut myself off from the Church, I didn't know what was happening. When I came back, I found a different kind of Church. The Church wasn't belly button gazing; it was examining itself in light of the contemporary experience of man. It came alive for me, personally. I felt that I might have a place in it, that I might be creative and active — that I might be a priest.

In the pre-Vatican II Church, I was like a lot of other people. I considered myself a very good Catholic. I was at the Sacrament of Penance almost every other week, Communion frequently during the week, Mass on Sunday. I mean, I was a rule-following Catholic. Underneath, there was some real faith in action, a love of God, but I still think I saw my love of God in terms of the practice of the law. A good Pharisee I was.

But I had really gone through a metamorphosis. From a conservative upstate Catholic, I was now a blooming liberal radical. My personality had changed, my whole outlook had changed: I had become a different person. And the new me was not conservative.

That's where my roots were. Gloversville, which is about

twenty miles north and west of Albany, wasn't much bigger than the size of the parish I'm in now. It was a nice place to grow up. Everybody knew everybody. And Dad was a businessman, so I got to know a lot of people. He was a Greek immigrant and, like all Greek immigrants, he opened a restaurant. We were a family that went to Mass on Sunday, didn't eat meat on Friday, said grace before meals; but there was nothing unusual about us, even as traditional Catholics.

When I was about in the sixth grade, I really expressed an interest in becoming a priest. I would go to Church on Sunday and *observe* the Mass — because it was in Latin, I really don't think I could *participate*. But there was something godly, something holy, about it, and my attitude toward the priest was probably what we call "hero worship."

The feeling continued and, at the end of my sophomore year in high school, I asked if I could go to a Catholic school — I had gone to a public school till then. That would test my desire to be a priest. Well, I graduated from high school in 1958 and entered the minor seminary for the Diocese of Albany.

I lasted about six months. I went there with a certain sense of idealism. This was going to be the brotherhood where everyone enjoyed serving everyone else. You know, the Kingdom on earth. I found out that the seminary was just as trying as a regular college: people were not perfect and, in fact, there were a lot of problems. I decided that this was not what I was cut out to be. I left and put the idea of priesthood out of my mind.

I worked for a year in the restaurant at home. Then, in September of '59 I went to Le Moyne College, a Jesuit college in Syracuse. In the time I was there, my theology instructor was Father Daniel Berrigan. He was teaching Pope John's encyclical *Mater et Magistra*. Now, here I was, this upstate, Republican conservative, and along comes this wonderful social encyclical encouraging cooperation among the nations, acceptance of global responsibilities, awareness of man's obligations to others. And Father Berrigan was suggesting that not only should we give rice to the Chinese but that we should also give them the atomic bomb because, in that way, we could visibly demonstrate our friendly ties to them. And, of course, we shouted: "You're mad! You're a Communist!" It was a very volatile class. He didn't mean this literally, of course. It was his style of teaching. He wanted us to criticize his remarks, you know. That's the kind of man he was. He saw the vision and cast it before the students. In a real sense, that's fulfilling the prophetic mission of the Church. Even if nothing happens as a result of the word being spoken, at least the word continues to be spoken.

The way I felt about Daniel Berrigan then is certainly not the way I feel about him today. I've emerged into a more cosmopolitan person, a person who is sensitized by needs that extend beyond my own. I think, basically, the problem is selfishness. I think selfishness is one of the real sins of the time. This vocation, the priesthood, speaks against that. I think that's one of the attractions it has for me.

I think the four years at Le Moyne College were the happiest in my life. Primarily, the experience away from home was good. But also it was a place where I really began to form myself as a person. I was exploring all different kinds of thoughts and ideas; I was really getting into life, and finding out who I was — a very good person, creative, politically aware, a person in tune with life.

When I left college, I came to New York. And I gave up the practice of the faith. It was easy. In college there was community, but when I left college, there was no real support. In cities there's always a certain anonymity. I didn't know anybody in New York who was going to church.

Also, my life was very social. Here I was, a small-town dude who had come to the big city. It was exciting and everything was happening and I loved it. And then I got involved in a relationship with a young woman. Having been a rule-following Catholic, I could never be in this situation and still go to church; so I chose to give up the practice of my faith.

I got a job with the New York Family Hospital as a case aide in the intake department. I was doing work with children who were admitted to the institution as various police-aided cases. Some of these children had been abandoned at home, for example. Some had mothers who'd been taken to a hospital for emergency surgery or had had a heart attack. In other words, children who were in need of care and had no immediate relative or agency to take them in.

The hospital had an agency that would board these children from infancy to two years. The children stayed there until, for example, Mommy got better. In some cases the situation called for longer-term foster home care and, ultimately, adoption. But those cases were few.

My job was contact with the child, the agencies, the mother —just kind of be an overseer in this crisis situation.

And then, in 1965, they began a pilot project placing children in private foster homes. Instead of sending them upstairs to a nursery, we would place them with a family immediately. That involved twenty-three foster homes in the five boroughs and Westchester. So I did quite a bit of traveling in '65 and '66. There were all kinds of coordinating services to provide medical check-ups for the child, and things like that.

I enjoyed it and I did very well at the job, but when it came to the dictation, getting it down on paper, I was a failure. At one point, I had about three hundred cases that I hadn't dictated out. The worker has the responsibility to make entries in a log for each child. Every time there was a contact, there was supposed to be an entry. I was worried about that and felt I needed another job.

I moved to casework with the Youth Counsel Bureau. This agency began because the five district attorneys of the city got together and suggested a probation-like experience for first offenders for minor infractions of the law. This was for kids sixteen to twenty-one. We would take the kids and have them for three months of casework and supervision. Get to know the boy or girl, the family, what the situation was at home. Was the child a potential criminal? Was he really a good kid who was hanging around with the wrong people at the wrong time? We'd make a recommendation, and then the district attorney would have the option of prosecuting or not prosecuting.

The average case was a sixteen-year-old kid caught smoking

a joint of marijuana in some public area. Or a kid jumping the turnstyle in the subway. Some of the more serious cases involved parents who would bring the child to court and charge him or her with disobedience and being a wayward minor. But, almost without exception, these were good kids who had just done something really stupid. The district attorney recognized that, the parents recognized that, so did the cops and the social workers. The point was to try to teach the kid that to commit a crime is trouble. It was an opportunity for a good kid to redeem himself. And that's why I liked the work. It was really good.

I did that from '66 to '70. Now during 1963 and up to '65, something very significant was happening to the Church, and even though I wasn't going to Mass, I was aware of what was going on — the Second Vatican Council. But there was still a little bit of Republican upstate conservative in me that said I didn't like these changes. My old rule-following mentality kept saying: "You can't be changing things." So it wasn't just the other things that kept me away from the Church. Part of it was based on disturbance of those traditions that I thought were sacred and holy and untouchable.

In '67 I broke the engagement with my girl friend. I just did not want to accept the responsibility of a wife and family. I knew that clearly. It was a nice vision, but I did not see myself fitting into it. Breaking it off was traumatic. I don't think two people who love one another can walk away from that love without being traumatized. And I loved her, deeply, intimately.

After that, through my work, two priests came into my life. Probably neither of them was outstanding for any one thing or other. Just two good priests. So I had this marginal contact with the Church during this time. I would occasionally go to a Mass because I knew the priest. It was a very personal thing.

Well, in 1968, a distant great-aunt of my mother's died, and we all went over to Montclair, New Jersey, for the funeral. This was the first time since the Second Vatican Council that I'd been in a Catholic church for a funeral Mass.

I remember, as an altar boy when I was young ... there was the priest in black vestments, the *Dies Irae* ... all very somber, very ... black. So now I come into a church and see a white cover over the casket, a priest in white vestments, Mass in English, with the priest facing the people—I felt like a foreigner! This was a whole new bag for me.

But something else. Going to church for me meant standing at the right time, kneeling at the right time, following the rules. I'd follow along with the prayers, but the really important thing was doing the right thing at the right time. Well, my family, not being that religious, didn't know whether to stand or to sit or to kneel. Half of us were doing one thing, half another. And here was this priest who could obviously see we were floundering, and he wouldn't help us out. I thought: "Look at this dumb ass. No wonder I don't like priests. What a stupid jerk he is." I was very angry.

In the middle of my anger, my conscience — I prefer to say the voice of God — called me and said, "Well, there's no reason, George, why you can't do what he is not doing." And I said: "Get away from me! Go away! I did that when I was young. I don't need any part of that nonsense."

Well, the Mass and the burial got over with, but it was two months later and I still couldn't stop thinking about it. I could not escape that call: *There's no reason, George, why you can't do what he is not doing.* So I went to one of the priests and said: "Now look, I know this is going to sound crazy. I know you only see me as a nonpracticing Catholic, but I really think there's something serious in this. Maybe I should think about it."

He said: "Absolutely not. Give it up. Don't even think about it twice."

So I went to the other priest and he said, "Well, maybe you're right." So I had to make the decision. It had to be mine. And I think that's the way it has to be. Each man must say yes to God. Nobody else can do it for you.

After that funeral I began to practice the faith again. I went on a retreat, and a seminarian told me about Pope John Seminary. "Give it a chance," I thought. "If I'm rejected, I'll get my master's and make my career in social work." So I applied to the seminary in '69, and in '70 I was accepted for the fall.

71

I must say I closed no door behind me in the world. I took a year's leave of absence from my job. My sister moved into my apartment, with the understanding that if I came back, I would move back and resume my life again.

My father said nothing, my mother said I was crazy, my sister said, "Well, if that's what's going to make you happy, maybe you ought to try it." For the most part, my friends said, "No way! Not you!" Most people were just indifferent.

It was in the seminary that I really learned about the new Church — through the studying I did, through reading the documents of Vatican II, through the men who taught me and the men with whom I lived at the seminary. I think all those things came together to give me a vision of God's kingdom.

I really found a different kind of Church.

I don't mean to make it sound like a totally different Church. I'm a Roman Catholic and I'm proud to be a Roman Catholic. I believe that the Roman Catholic Church has within its structure, within its reality, the truest tradition of Jesus Christ in the world today. And tradition is very persuasive for me. But I also think that God has given us this time and this place to help the Church to vitality, to challenge it, to keep it alive.

You know, there is no better time than right now to be a priest. I wouldn't ever want to be anything other than a priest. I feel very happy, very fulfilled as a priest. My life has taken on the meaning that it should. It is the best vocation in the world.

When I went to the seminary after high school, I don't think I wanted to be a priest, actually. I think I wanted the glamor of the priesthood, the title, the honor. When I read Matthew twenty-three about the Pharisees, I always get scared because it reminds me of me then: "All their works are performed to be seen.... They are fond of places of honor at banquets and the front seats in synagogues."

I think that's what I wanted to be, the selfish me. But not the second time. I think my own egoism about the priesthood had been tempered and I'd really come to understand it in a much different way, a way that includes more of the cross, more of the spiritual reality ... less of the temporary and more of the eternal.

Through that dramatic event in which I felt that God was acting in my life, I have changed. I'm less of a Pharisee now, more of a compassionate person; a priest who is not afraid to say that he is a sinner, who admits his weaknesses, who acknowledges that he has made mistakes, who can say he's sorry. I have more of a servant mentality now; whereas, before, I was a pompous ass.

There's still a part of me that doesn't like the role of the servant, you know. The selfish part of me says, "Ah, come on. Don't do that — don't give up your day off and bring Communion to that old lady on Eighty-first Street!" But yet ... I'm a priest: I do it.

I think I'll have struggles all my life. Yes ... but not ones that I can't cope with, not extraordinary ones. Just frustrations.

I have a personal relationship with the Lord. That's the key, I think. This is the age of personalism. If there ever was a time when the Church meant anything, it means people, and people to people. That is how God acts — through people. And anyone who can't discover people, who is so closed to others, is missing the understanding of the contemporary Church.

As a priest, I'm called to leadership in the Church by the Orders that I have received. But, in Baptism, each one of us is called to the priesthood of the faithful. I've been called to fill a certain place and role in the Church, but the more important call, the more important election, was the election at Baptism.

There is no greater privilege for me than to say the prayer of Jesus at the Eucharist. There is no greater privilege than to serve God's people in sacramental ways. There is no greater gift in life than the gift of God's love, and to be a little instrument in that is to continue God's love in the world.

The priesthood places one in touch with people throughout their whole lives and at critical points in their lives. I can think of no other vocation where in a single day one can touch life at its beginning, at marriage, at death. That was the most outstanding attraction for me.

THOMAS BURR

A Climber Discovers a New Plane

"I played the corporate game, and, as a priest today, I talk about some of the elements of that game. I've had some practical experience, and I have a pretty good idea of what that game is. I think I played it pretty well. The expense account game. The contact game. The visibility game. The upward-mobility game. I studied it, and I think I know a little bit about how the corporate life can affect people, what it can do to them."

His office in the rectory is small, crowded, with a desk covered with stacks of papers and files. But once, Thomas Burr was living the corporate life. He was on the rise in the Continental Casualty Company of Chicago. He became a regional sales manager, traveling five days a week most of the year, living on expense accounts.

He liked the competition, the challenge to succeed, the thrill and excitement of winning. But slowly and subtly he began to reassess his own values. He found that he wasn't so sure of the goals he had when he began in the company. There were parts of his life that weren't really fulfilling. When he was thirty-three, he entered Pope John XXIII National Seminary in Weston, Massachusetts, to study to become a priest.

Now an associate pastor at St. Laurence Church in Elgin, Illinois, he finds that his ministry is reaching beyond parish lines. He is a chaplain with the Elgin Police Department, a campus minister at Elgin Community College. He is president of the board of directors of the Community Crisis Center, an organization dealing with domestic violence. When he received the Cosmopolitan Club's Distinguished Service Award in 1979, he said: "Part of ... everything that I do is my concern that we're losing our ability to take time and listen and care about others."

Burr confesses, with a slight nervous grin, that he doesn't know where his life is leading, and he admits to being scared at times. There are still many elements of his former self in his life; after all, no one changes personality by putting on a Roman collar. He admits to still being ambitious. Though his goals are different now, he is still definitely achievement-oriented, a fact that troubles him at times. He enjoys being in control. Only slowly is he relinquishing control to God, and he finds the process painful...

I was terribly ambitious. At Continental, I became conscious of entering the upward-mobility race. I can remember being very aware of the need for being seen down in the bar after work, being visible to the chairman of the board and the various vice-presidents.

Shortly after I went there, Continental went through a change of the chairman of the board and some of the vice-presidents. There were a few other purges also at this time, so there was a lot of jockeying. I became somewhat of a student of the great upward-mobility scramble. Do you know the musical *How to Succeed in Business Without Really Trying*? Well, there was an element of that in my life. I wanted to climb.

You'd go to a cocktail party and watch who was talking to whom, what corner of the balcony or apartment they were in. Then you'd try to figure out what was going on. I watched whom people invited to their Christmas party and, perhaps even more important, whom they didn't invite. I watched the wives too, how some of them maneuvered. There were a few wives who were as vicious as the men, probably more so. I became very aware of the competition between vice-presidents and assistant vice-presidents of the various divisions, observing their scramble to move up the ladder. I wasn't in their league ... but I wasn't too far behind.

It was kind of exciting to play the game. It was a form of Russian roulette. You couldn't afford to make many wrong moves. You couldn't be seen with the wrong people. Part of the challenge was the money, but part of it was the game itself, the competition, watching other people, how they operated.

I don't think I ever knowingly stepped on another guy's back. I don't like to think of myself as a user of people, but I probably did do that to some small degree. I didn't intend to: I wanted to compete with them.

But there were some instances in which I saw men used badly, very badly, by their bosses or their peers. Many of these people are good people, I would maintain, but I think their values are messed up. Looking back, I suppose some of them realized it along the way.

But it's important that I not be too judgmental. These people were and are friends of mine. Basically, they are good people. I know that sounds contradictory, but they are good. Now that I'm out of corporate life, I see that our values differ — it's a bit like two different worlds.

From my observations, I slowly began to get a hint of what was happening in this pursuit of money and power. Part of it, I suppose, was the realization that quite a number of the men who enjoyed some success had disastrous marriages and homelives. Part of it, too, was the awareness that there were people who did their job honestly and as well as they could but didn't get caught up in this corporate climbing. These and other factors made me ask myself where I was going.

I realized that there was a kind of emptiness in my own life. It occurred to me that while others may be happy in corporate life, there might be something more for me in my life.

During this period, I was questioning. What was I doing here? What did I hope to gain? It was very subtle, sometimes only looking ahead to the future — was I going to spend the next forty years of my life commuting? Would I spend my life in this overall pattern?

Even though I was competitive — and still am competitive — I was questioning the system to some degree. I wasn't sure where it all led. I'd seen guys retire with certain fears and a certain emptiness. I'd say, "Is that the way I'm going to go?"

And I really couldn't decide if this was good or bad. But it made me look more inside of myself. What was I really doing? What did I really hope to gain?

Sometimes, there were fleeting thoughts about the priesthood, but I'd just dismiss them. I didn't think I could do it. Besides, I didn't think I was good enough, holy enough, prayerful enough ... what I thought I should be, you know ... the "good boy" image. I had idealized the priesthood ... my concept of it. This had built up over the years because of the priests I'd seen.

In some ways, too, I looked at priests as a little bit on the cloistered side. I'd seen priests who had stuck very close to their rectories, and I was a little afraid of that. I was a little afraid, probably, of people and their problems.

But one of the things that kept bringing the priesthood idea back was that, every third week in January, about twenty of us from Continental would go out to New Mallory, a Trappist monastery in Iowa, and make a retreat. I remember one time — scared the hell out of me — as we were leaving, one of the brothers, a guy as bald as I am, grabbed my hat and rubbed the top of my head and said, "We ought to keep you here; you're halfway here already." I almost died. He verbalized something that had been there but that I hadn't dared to verbalize for myself.

I was born and raised in St. Charles, Illinois, the third of four children. My younger brother died when I was about six or seven. My father worked for the State Bank of St. Charles for forty-eight years. We were what I would call "typical Catholics" — no meat on Friday, church every Sunday. We did all the things that good Catholics were supposed to do.

I went to Marmion Military Academy. It's run by the Benedictines ... an excellent college prep school. In my sophomore year I got interested in law and pretty much made up my mind to be an attorney, and from that time on I started looking at Georgetown University. So when I graduated from Marmion in 1953, I went to Georgetown undergraduate for four years, and then to Georgetown Law School until the fall of '59.

During my third year in college, I began dating one of the girls in the nursing school. We were fairly serious about getting married by the time we graduated, but the more we talked about it and the closer we were to setting a date, the more she realized marriage would interfere with her plans to be a nurse; and I realized that marriage might interfere with my plans for law school. So the engagement never really came off, and we just dated on and off after that. At a party in my apartment, I introduced her to a fellow who was a year ahead of me in law school and in the same law fraternity. Ten years later they got married and, believe it or not, we're still very good friends.

Anyway, in the fall of '59, I was running out of deferments from military service, and there was a new six-month reserve program. Well, after the military, I was tired of being broke, so I thought I would work for a year before going back to law school. I came back and went to work for the State Bank of Geneva, the next town over from St. Charles.

I worked there less than a year. My brother-in-law was helping to form a new bank in Arlington Heights, and the board of directors offered me a job there. I went in as a teller and later on became assistant vice-president, assistant cashier — something like that. I did all the loan work, a lot of FHA loans. We had phenomenal growth because of the location we were in, the hours we had, everything about it. It was a good job; it was exciting.

I left there after about four years. The five men who were officers had agreed not to take raises so we could keep the help we had ... at least for the first year or two. Well, I found out that one of the other fellows in loans, a guy who wasn't doing his job, got raises. I really was ticked off. When I confronted the board of directors, they said he was married and had a child, and I wasn't. Well, I told them what they could do with that, and gave them notice.

This was '63 or '64. I went to work for a broker I had dealt with who had formed his own brokerage. My job was to research underpriced stock situations. Having seen the hot issues pushed, he believed that with a little bit of work you could make some valid recommendations for your clients — buy, sell, sit tight, or whatever. He was a very sharp guy and a very moral person.

It was detective work, probably one of the most exciting jobs I've had. I did research on Brunswick, the bowling equipment manufacturer and Chock Full O' Nuts, which really came alive later on. The biggest one I researched was the New York, New Haven, Hartford Railroad. It was going into bankruptcy for the second time in twenty-five, thirty years. I worked three, four, maybe six months on that, traveling up and down the East Coast from Washington to New York to Hartford, New Haven, and Boston, trying to dig out what was going on. I couldn't confirm it, but I had a hunch the Penn Central merger was coming. I speculated that if the Penn Central and the New York Central were allowed to merge, the New York, New Haven would be part of the merger, too. It was a lucky guess — because that's what happened.

The man I was working for bought into a brokerage that had maybe twelve members. I think the youngest was sixty-two. They wanted to rely on the established analysis houses in New York instead of using me. They offered me a job, but it was pretty much back-room stuff. I wanted to work with people.

I stayed in Chicago and, through my boss, I got a job with Continental Casualty in what was called the Association Group Division. It had group policies, accident and health, not life, for professional associations. My first job was, again, statistical analysis. I would look at the overall performance of each group. Was it making a buck or not? I would try to analyze why or why not. It was, again, a detective kind of thing.

Later, I began traveling with my boss a little bit, talking to agents and associations. And then the division decided to decentralize the underwriting and claims systems. My job was to go to the major cities where we had branch offices and set up those systems. I went to New York, San Francisco, Dallas, and Kansas

City. But then management reversed the decision and we weren't decentralizing after all. I came back to Chicago.

At that time I was dating another gal very steadily, maybe six months. I had met Carol on a blind date. We had a lot of fun. We used to go up to what is now Old Town, but it wasn't so commercial then. Someone would bring a guitar or a banjo, and you could buy a pitcher of beer for eighty-five cents.

It was a strange thing. I think if her mother had not pushed, we would have gotten married. But she did, and it made me put on the brakes. I remember her mother bugged the hell out of me when I went to New York. Around Easter she wrote and said if I had any sense, we would get married right after Easter at St. Patrick's, my home parish in Illinois. Well, I was running scared, and though we kept dating, it wasn't as serious anymore.

One day I was on my way to Kansas City, on a flight out of O'Hare, and I grabbed a *Chicago Tribune*. Carol had been killed in a boating accident right off Navy Pier. She was with some other people. I don't understand it. She never even liked the water. Her mother blamed me for that — if we had been married this wouldn't have happened.

I went through a time of guilt. I knew, too, that if I had married her, it might never have happened. But it didn't last extremely long. I knew I liked her, but I knew I didn't want to marry her. And frankly, as I think back now, there may have been a feeling of relief.

I can't remember thinking about the priesthood when I was dating Carol. But, you know, that...that questioning continued. I shy away from the term *call* because, I think, at times it's overused, or inaccurately used. But I believe God was speaking to me, *calling* me, if you will, by moving me to question what I was doing. I think He was calling me to a different life-style. But, of course, I didn't recognize it as that at first. I wasn't sure it was a call. And I continued to question.

Back in Chicago, I was made a regional sales manager. I was responsible for all the states west of the Mississippi River. The premium income I was responsible for was fifty-six million dollars a year. It was my job to keep it profitable and to sell, but I did very little selling because I had a busy time just keeping it profitable.

I was a lot into the writing of the policies for the American Medical Association, the crown of the industry. The indemnities then were big money — five hundred, seven hundred and fifty, a thousand dollars a month.

Basically, I liked the job. I liked the travel. I met a lot of interesting people. It was challenging presenting a new case because, being the acknowledged leader, Continental was the target for many of the big companies. Very often I'd see another outfit come in and get a copy of our proposal and then simply cut the rate by ten percent ... or whatever.

Work was my big thing. I traveled fifty or fifty-two weeks a year, four or five days a week. And my basic reason was profit. I had the biggest premium income of the eight regional managers in that division. Gutsy, maneuvering, finagling — yeah, that was me.

I had a lot of friends all over the country — agents, executive directors of professional associations — a lot of good, intelligent, interesting people. I would leave on a Monday morning, and in the course of five days, I might cover Chicago, Kansas City, Dallas, San Francisco, and back to Chicago. All with absolutely no money out of my own pocket. Talk about playing the game ... okay? I never ate alone. I'd call an agent or executive secretary or somebody, and that was a valid expense account item. Of all the cities I was in, I can think of only a few times I ate alone. It was a kind of a life-style — extremely public, business-oriented, achievement-oriented.

Sometimes I'd be host at cocktail parties for associations. I mean, you'd slosh up the boys and give them a little spiel. You know, a freebie drink and they'd buy anything. That sounds cynical, but it was also part of that game.

Often I'd spend weekends in Colorado. I love skiing. I met a guy who had a condominium north of Breckenridge, so usually during the skiing season I'd manage to end up in Denver on Friday. No one kept that close a tab on me ... as long as I kept my region profitable.

But it got to the point where I realized that the way things were set up in the Association Group Division, any advancement for me was absolutely stymied. So it was probably one of the few times I actually asked for and maneuvered for a change. A friend of mine at that time was in what was called the Reinsurance and International Division, and he was moving out into another division. I went after his job and I got it.

My job there was basically helping with the negotiations with Lloyds of London — rates, what coverages we would write or not write, whether to pick up a percent of a contract or a treaty — very much the statistical end of things. I was in the reinsurance division for something short of two years. That takes us up to the fall of '69. I quit Continental and entered Pope John XXIII.

Jack, an associate pastor at my parish, St. Pat's, had gotten me to teach CCD. One night, we were talking, having a drink, and he asked me if I was thinking about being a priest. I said yes. But I told him not to crowd me because I wasn't ready for a decision. He respected that. But he asked me to make a retreat with the seminarians from the Rockford diocese. So I did, and I met a couple of guys who had entered the seminary later than others. And I really bounced a lot of questions off them. That helped me to some degree, but it was another year before I actually decided. In that year I didn't want people to make a big thing of it. I didn't want them to start knitting little black things. If Jack had pushed me, I probably wouldn't have gone.

You have to realize that I considered myself very definitely a very average Catholic. Typically, I didn't take too many chances with God, but at the same time I was far from being what you'd call a religious person. I did the minimal kind of thing. I didn't bother Him and He didn't bother me. Our relationship was cordial ... but distant.

When this priesthood thing started, I wanted it to go away — I really did. I remember one night I got bombed. I was in tears over this thing. It was inconvenient and there were times I'd do a pretty good job of suppressing the idea entirely. And I can't tell you just what would trigger it, but there I'd be thinking about it again.

At first, I wasn't that sure that God had picked me. It was a matter of try-it-and-see. If it didn't work out, then I could really dismiss the damn thing. And if it came up again, I could say I had tried it, and get off my back. But I'd never know if I didn't try. It was really with that kind of approach that I decided to enter a seminary.

Yes, it was painful. I was afraid of having to give up too much. I had a certain amount of financial security, a certain amount of status, a certain amount of satisfaction. While I didn't necessarily lose those things, the pain was partly the unknown. At least I knew what I had.

But I was attracted to the priesthood somewhat instinctively because of the helping aspect of it, the personalism of it. I was afraid of it, I found it somewhat irresistible. I saw it as, well ... doing good things. Though I was attracted to that, I did not see it as my personal ticket to heaven, however. I thought of it as maybe changing some of the things I didn't like in the society I saw.

I left Continental very quietly. Some people were very surprised. Some couldn't comprehend it. Afterwards I got letters that were hysterically funny; people just couldn't imagine me in a seminary.

The first year — two years actually — at Pope John, I had a lot of really anxious times. I thought of dropping out. There were times when I thought I'd made the dumbest, most disastrous mistake of my life. At times I found it comical. At times I missed what I now call my former life. But the other piece of that was the whole reevaluation of life that I was going through.

One factor that helped was the support from other people there. There were six of us called the Irish Mafia. When we first got to the seminary, we weren't supposed to have booze in our rooms. Well, all of us had a bottle ... we all did. We were like kids — we'd hide it. In my freshman year, though, they lifted the ban. Well, the Irish Mafia discovered that if we went up to New Hampshire, the booze was a lot cheaper. So we'd go up there and buy it by the half gallon. There was a room that wasn't being used, and we'd store it all in there. Just about every day, after

Mass and before dinner, we'd usually meet in there and have a drink. That was the support system. If you were down or ticked off or whatever, you'd kind of rap about that.

There were times when I resented having to watch the money. Here I'd been traveling and living on expense accounts; now I had to watch it. We were close to Regis College, so some of us got jobs as dorm daddies on weekends. We'd stand at the door as the kids came in and out. I guess they paid us two-fifty an hour. That was a little bit of income.

I was ordained in Rockford on June 9, 1973, and served two years at Our Lady of Good Counsel in Aurora as associate pastor. Three years ago this coming July, I moved up here.

I still sometimes think I've made a disastrous mistake. Every day is not peaches and cream. I don't wake up in the morning and think, "Oh goody, I'm a priest!" At times it's very disillusioning, very discouraging. Disillusionment more than discouragement. With me, with my decisions, with people.

There are pains. Oh yeah, I'd give my eyeteeth to bolt out of here sometimes for a long weekend and go skiing. Not always. But, you know, that's part of me. It's not as strong as before. There will always be some very pleasant memories. They fade, but they still make up a part of who I am. It's part of accepting myself.

I get scared sometimes because I don't know what's going to happen. And the control wants to know. I'm still, you know, a control type of person — to the point where, at times, I want God to give me some very clear signs as to what the hell is going on. Because I don't know.

I've changed in my spiritual life. Definitely. There has been a growing appreciation of prayer in my life. It's been slow, very slow. I'm learning to be content, learning to stop and smell the flowers. I don't know where this is going to lead, but I know that I have a stronger trust in God. As long as I'm open to God, somehow these things will take care of themselves. Yes, there's been growth.

I try to pray every day. My prayer now is in the form of a journal. I try to spend twenty minutes or more at my journal, which for me is a pretty good form of prayer. I address a love letter to the Father. I chew Him out. I tell Him to get the hell out of the way. That's why I can't say I've changed that much over the years. I still want to be in control of God. But I trust Him more than I ever did before, and slowly and subtly I'm letting Him be in control of me. It doesn't stop my fears; it helps me deal with them. But I may write God about how frightened I am, in terms of what I'm doing, why am I here.

One of the most rewarding things about priesthood is the depth to which people allow me into their lives. That's very, very inspirational to me. Pretty different from my experiences when I was with Continental. That was very superficial. At times it's frightening. I don't know of anyone else who has this. Even psychiatrists are not allowed into some of those areas. That's a particularly exciting aspect of being a priest that I've only come to realize in the last couple of years. But there's a real cost, a real price to pay. I'm giving up a lot of myself.

I find myself now moving into other ministries. And I didn't set out for this, I really didn't. Working as a police chaplain, I'm very conscious of the divorce rate, of family problems, of guys beating their wives. Working with students, I see a real need for ministry in this area. A priest should be there, have coffee with them, rap with them, argue with them sometimes. The further I get into these nonparish things — at least not immediately identified with a parish — I see a crying need for a ministry other than in parochial terms, as we now define it.

Sometimes it's depressing because of the overwhelming needs and the awesomeness of it all. In battering situations, for example, you can get all caught up in the inadequacy of laws and the courts. At times people get very uncomfortable when a priest is working in this area, when he talks about, oh, say, getting a woman benefits from her husband. And sometimes both Catholics and non-Catholics wonder what the hell is a priest doing in that area in the first place. They're very uncomfortable with that. You know: "Go home to your rectory, Father." I just smile.

I really believe the Church should be walking that incredible razor's edge of being *in* the world but not *of* it. And that's where I see myself now. Sometimes I get hard on myself because I see myself as too much of a social worker, not enough the man of prayer. At other times I think maybe I'm closer to the balance. But that's so fluid that I can never say I'm right on the money. But I'm not always unhappy with my efforts at balance.

I know I can relate to people more because of my previous life. I can relate to them because I've learned to listen with my heart more than I ever did before. I can help them identify. Maybe I can say, "I've been there." Granted that this is the age of personalism, but if you're going to be in the now, in the present time, in the modern world, then you've got to be able to hang on to a lot of the facts of what's going on.

As a priest, I think I'm special — but I'm not better. I think I have a gift to offer. Everyone has a gift to offer. Part of my gift is to be a priest.

For example, celibacy is a gift that I give to people. I don't mean that as a pat answer. In being celibate I'm free to love many others. I'd vote for the option, but I'd never marry: I think it would be unfair to my wife; I think it would be restrictive to my ministry. Yes, there are sexual problems. I'm very human. There are times when I get turned on, have the horny moments. I wish I were somehow an angel and didn't have that kind of distraction. But I don't have a big problem dealing with my own sexuality, and I'm not afraid of it. But I'm very conscious of the line. I'm very aware of being turned on at times, and there are times when I'd like to have the sexual gratification. Definitely. But I had to buy into some of those rules, and it's taken me to this time to work through to the point where I'm at.

The biggest problem for me is that I will never have my own child. I don't know why it's a problem. I suppose just the drive to reproduce myself ... to give life. I've opted to live with it. I don't know how long it will be there, but it was a choice I made.

One of the things I've decided to do very recently is to get myself a counselor, another priest. Because I do at times need help. I need someone to bounce my problems off of too. Not that I have any enormous problems. I just need someone with whom I can share those deeper areas. It may be an indication of the loneliness of priesthood, but I think it's just a growing awareness of my own need to be supported, to communicate in a role other than many people see me. Instead of always being the helper, I'm the one who needs the help sometimes.

Part of the need for counseling is the need to communicate in depth, to be appreciated and affirmed. I analyze myself a lot, yes. Basically, I don't have a good self-image, but it's improving. I used to worry that I would not be able to measure up as a priest. Some days I think I've probably measured up beyond my expectations — but I still don't measure up because what I expect of myself constantly increases. I'm probably very afraid of becoming complacent. I like change. I like moving around. I'm not afraid of growing old, but I'm afraid of stagnating as I've seen a lot of priests do.

Part of the excitement of living, of being a priest, is being sensitive to where I'm at, what's going on with me, how I'm interacting with people. At times it's very scary. Part of me is trying to give up control. That's slow ... I may die and not make a hell of a lot of progress on that. I think I've got a long way to go, but that's part of being alive.

JOSEPH GANNON

A Salesman for God

"Why did I want to be a priest? I guess I'd answer that by saying I didn't want to be one. But something told me, 'Yes, you ought to do this.' I think there is something to a calling. It seemed to me that there was an opportunity that opened up to me. Not that I was sure I would make it. In fact I thought I probably wouldn't. But I had to try.

"I had a lot of excuses, but then I ran out of them. I mean, you certainly wouldn't ask to have your wife die, but she had died. The children were raised, the business was going well: everything was right. So here was an opportunity. I had to face it. I just ran out of excuses. It wasn't a struggle ... a real struggle."

It's one of those crisp winter mornings that Minnesota is famous for, and in the lake country north of Minneapolis and St. Paul, the study of St. Peter's Church is warm and cozy. Father Joseph Gannon's parish spreads over two hundred square miles out of the community of Forest Lake. Gannon says that he can't just tell a parishioner that he'll "run over to your house tonight."

Most of the parishioners work in the Twin Cities, once the base for Gannon himself. He says he was "just a business salesman," but actually he owned a profitable company that franchised doughnut machines and mixes. And before that, he operated Gannon's Restaurants.

Gannon had grown up in the Depression, one of nine children, into a comfortable life. He and his wife watched as their own six children grew up, and soon there were ten grandchildren. They looked forward, as Gannon says, to growing old and rocking in their chairs. But, after thirty-five years of marriage, Gannon's wife died of cancer.

A year later, at fifty-six, he entered the Beda College in Rome, an institution designed for former Anglican priests and older vocations to the Catholic priesthood. And when he was sixty, he was ordained by Pope Paul VI...

I think some time you think about things subconsciously and you don't realize it. A lot of people said they weren't surprised when I said I was going to be a priest. It surprised me that they said it.

And it wasn't that I was just bringing it up then. My wife sometimes asked me what I would do if something happened to her. And I'd say I'd probably go back to school, and perhaps look into a seminary. "Oh," she'd say, "you'll be married in thirty days." I'd say, no, that there would be an opportunity to consider the priesthood if that ever happened. Not that I wasn't happily married. But I never thought that anything would ever happen to her.

She didn't feel threatened by this. She just thought I was trying to make points with her because she thought I'd get married. She'd say, "You'll find some floozy and I hope you get one that will keep the house absolutely perfect." I always was kind of a fuddy-duddy. Kind of stems out of the Depression, I think. When you buy something, you feel that you have to keep it good. The house, the furniture, and so forth. She understood that. She came out of the Depression too.

The Depression was hard. There were nine of us children, each of us a year apart, except for two, and they were ten months apart. I was the oldest boy, and I had one older sister. I had five brothers and three sisters.

We lived in Farmington, about thirty miles out of Minneapolis and St. Paul. My dad was ... well, what you call a contractor; but he was more into repair, remodeling, and painting, and such things. He didn't get much work during the Depression, so we did many things to make it work out. When the milkman — they delivered in those days — came in from the farm, the first place he delivered was our house. Two of us boys would go and help him deliver his route. And then on Saturdays we'd go out and clean the barns. And when the milkman needed a haircut, my dad would cut his hair. So we got our milk free.

And then for coal and flour, when a carload of coal came into the elevator, whoever was old enough would go down and throw the coal off. None of us was big enough to look over the side of the car rack. And for this we would get our coal and our flour from the elevator.

Then my mother would take the flour and make angel food cakes. You might wonder where we got the eggs, because it takes so many eggs. Well, there was a farm right near us, and we'd go out and help them put down hay for the cows and clean the barns, and we'd get our eggs from them.

My mother would make angel food cakes and doughnuts, and we'd pack the doughnuts in half-dozen bags and put them all in a wagon and go over to what we called the silk-stocking side of town and sell what she made. I always said it was the sadness in our faces that helped us sell them, but she was a good baker. And she made homemade bread, and we'd sell that to the people also. We'd just go door to door.

And then my father finally got on WPA, the federal work program. You saw lots of people working like that. I remember seeing the man who owned the big jewelry store in town shoveling snow for the city. When I asked about that, my mother said he had to close the store. Well, you know, who would buy jewelry at a time like that?

We look back now, it was tough. But we were getting along. There were a lot of days, though, we just had cornmeal mush, and that's a fact. We had it for breakfast, and we didn't bother with eating at noon a lot of times ... and, you know, through the years, I hardly stop to eat at noon. For dinner then we'd have eggs and mashed potatoes, or more cornmeal mush.

Well, when I got out of high school, I started working for the gas company. They were putting gas in towns in southern Minnesota. In 1940 I was made a manager, and they asked me to go to Iowa. I was married by then, so my wife and I moved to Lake Mills, Iowa. I was in the distribution part of it. When the gas was brought into the town, the manager had to see that the lines got out into the homes.

I always had an idea of being in business for myself. I started thinking about it more and more and decided to leave the gas company. I bought the restaurant right next door to the office. I remember when I called the vice-president in Omaha and told him what I was going to do, and he said I couldn't boil water. "Well," I said, "I know that, but I want to give it a chance."

So I bought a restaurant. The man who owned it arranged some easy terms for me. He had to if he wanted to sell it, because I didn't have that kind of cash. I remember I started with the gas company at eighty dollars a month — even at that, we saved five dollars a month — and gradually I got up to a hundred and even a hundred and ten.

I opened the restaurant the day I was thirty in 1944. "The Grand Cafe." It took off like a big bird. We could seat about eighty downstairs and about fifty or sixty upstairs. We really packed them in. I remember one time I had to get the contractors out there to look at the structure of the floors because I worried that they would cave in. We had a soda fountain that was real long, and we'd get the kids after all the games.

We operated that restaurant for about two and a half years. I didn't have to go into the war. With the gas company I was classified as a key man. When I went into the restaurant business I was made Class A, but then they decided they weren't going to take men with children. By then I had two children.

I kept in contact with the gas company. Still had friends there. You know, I ran the restaurant but talked gas company. Finally I sold the restaurant for double what I paid for it. The gas company heard about it and asked me to come back. So I went down to Webster City, Iowa, and helped install the system there.

By the end of the fall, they saw I wasn't happy. I guess it was going into business for myself that kind of spoiled it for me. Well, I left the gas company and looked into clothing, hardware, and motels. There was a building available in Lake Mills, so I decided to open up a small fast-food place. No booths, all counter. Well, I remodeled that, with a lot of hardship, and got it opened. Standing room only. Weeks before it opened they were putting their heads in the door asking when it would open. It turned out to be an absolute natural. It was just an ideal spot for truckers, right on the highway and right on top of a hill. It was easy for them to stop. There was nothing else open for miles and miles, and we were open until three in the morning. We did real well, and of course overhead was down because I needed less help. The restaurant's there yet, and it's still the money-maker in town.

We operated that until 1950, I guess, and then I went to Osage, Iowa, and operated an A&W drive-in. Bought a restaurant in downtown Osage too.

Then a company came out with an automatic doughnut machine. They were selling territories and franchises. I sold the restaurant in Osage and bought a franchise in Minnesota. This was in Minneapolis. They were struggling at the time, but it looked like there were some possibilities. We had automatic machines, which we installed, and we provided the mixes that go with them. We sold them mostly to restaurants and existing food operations.

We operated in Minnesota, and some in the Dakotas. We only had a couple of salesmen, a couple of men in the plant, and a couple girls in the office. Friends of mine always said if you're going to get out of the restaurant business, go into some aspect of manufacturing that'll keep the help down.

I was on the road a lot, just beating the bushes. I had to — because we couldn't fail. And I knew if we could get out a hundred machines, they'd be ordering the mixes. And we were out looking for those orders. Well, the business took hold. Finally, I got enough new accounts and the mix load got bigger and people were reordering and reordering.

It was in 1970 that my wife contracted cancer. She hadn't been sick a day, but she felt swelled up on her breast and side, and she went into the hospital, where they operated. That was in August; in May she died. May 7, it was, just a week before our anniversary. She was only fifty-three, and we had been married thirty-five years.

I had known Arlene for so long. We went all the way through school together. She was three years younger, and I always knew her family. Her dad was a barber in our town.

Her family was Lutheran, and we were married in the Catholic rectory in Farmington. In those days you couldn't be married in the church. Everybody thought she was a Catholic. She belonged to everything and went to church. She was the first one to lead the rosary when we started trips in the car.

She became a Catholic some years after we were married. I think she always felt she would hurt her parents if she changed over. But when she decided, she told her mother, and her mother said she couldn't understand why she hadn't done that years ago. I'm still real close to her mother. I say to her: "You didn't think you'd end up with me, did you? And a Catholic priest on top of it!"

We knew it was going to be terminal. We prayed an awful lot, not that she would be cured — we faced that — but just that we had God's good will in everything that we did. — *God, You know what You're doing and Your will be done*. Well, finally, she went into a coma and, three days later, she died.

We had a good marriage. I always thought we'd just end up as eighty-year-olds in our chairs, rocking and enjoying our kids. There are lonely and sad times. They still come, you know. You see a sunset and you're used to saying, "Isn't that great!" Who do you say it to now? But as I go along — it's eight years now — my perspective changes. I start to see me going to her rather than wishing that she was back here. I wouldn't wish her back here for the world. Why? Unless you're going to live forever, there's no point.

Well, after my wife died, I thought I ought to get out of the business. I had two sons with me in the plant then. Tom was out of college, and Denny had been in the Navy Air Corps. They were saying that they couldn't try anything new because I wouldn't let them.

About a year later I heard a talk at a Serra Club meeting by a man from Wisconsin who had entered the priesthood late. Well, that started me thinking, you know, about what I had told my wife. So I talked to the vocations director here and to the archbishop and sent an application to Pope John Seminary in Massachusetts. But they said that because I had the boy, my youngest son, Mark, who was fourteen, they couldn't consider the application at that time. I had to get him through high school first. "Well," I thought, "fine. That's the Lord speaking. He doesn't want me."

And then I was kind of thinking about remarrying. I was noticing the lack of companionship and the loneliness. My son and I had the house by ourselves, this big house on Lake Nakomis. I started to have dinner with some gals, some that had lost their husbands and that Arlene and I had known for a long time. But I always let them know that I had the idea of the priesthood in mind — especially if I thought that they had some serious thoughts about remarrying. I suppose I was trying to be halfway honest.

The archbishop's office said they'd send an application to the Beda College in Rome. They replied that they were filled up, but if they had a cancellation they would notify us. So I figured, "That's it." I really started to put it out of my mind. There's no way. This tells me something. I thought I'd get on with it. Just get married...I didn't know.

Two weeks later we received a telegram from the Beda College. There'd been a cancellation, it said, and I should be there by October 30, which would give me, I guess, three weeks. So now I had to face it. I mean, I was going into a seminary. Before I was just kind of talking, you know how you do without even thinking about it. And I thought, "Boy, what have I done?"

"Well," I thought, "this is an opportunity. I've got to try it. If I don't, I'll always wonder if I should have done it."

But I kept thinking of excuses. I had just three weeks to sell my house, sell my mother's house, take care of my business, and take care of Mark. Well, the man next door offered to buy my mother's house, just like that. My sister bought my house. The business ... well, my two sons said I should put them on salary. They'd run it for a year and then we'd take a look at it. My daughter said she'd take Mark. So, just like that, I was on a plane going to Rome. Everything buttoned up.

The first few months were bad news. I was in with men of all kinds — men who had degrees from Oxford and Cambridge, architects and civil engineers. We had four doctors, one of them had been knighted by the queen. He was a surgeon. It didn't take me long to see that I was in with the majors when I should be back with the minors. I was just a business salesman, that's all. And, gradually, I just felt I was losing out. So I went to a professor and he said: "Just forget it. Some of those men will never make parish priests. Some of them won't even get through. You're not going to teach, you're going to be a parish priest."

I packed eight times. I'd go up in the loft, bring the trunk down, and I'd pack. Friends would say, "You can't do it. You're foolish." One man came in ... an Anglican priest, younger than I, only thirty. "You're greedy," he said. "You're packing up because you want what everyone else has got. A lot of us wish we had the stuff you have, but you don't recognize that."

And I was kind of like that. If I felt I couldn't do that well, I'd get low. You know ... the competition. All your life you've been beating out the competition, and here ... well, I worried a lot. Maybe because of my father. My father was a man who ... well, you didn't fail. Failure was one thing you didn't do.

I'd walk along the Tiber River and think and think. One afternoon the thought came to me to go home at Christmas and take a look at things. It would be expensive, but I felt I should do it. After that, I was just rarin' around there. I was just clickin'. In fact I got elected dean of the class — over all these men with all their degrees — and eventually wound up assistant dean of the college.

So I went home. Things were no different: the company was running, the family was fine. When I returned, I buckled down—

for two or three months. Then I got that feeling again. Just felt that I had made a mistake. I went down by the Tiber. I kept walking down there, talking out loud. "I'll go home for the summer," I figured. "I've spent a year here, given it a try."

After that, I didn't feel so cooped up. You know, I was on the fourth floor, with the light and a desk, a far cry from the home I had. I'd sit up in that little room and hear the big gates close at seven-thirty at night. Here I was, a person who had been at conventions, been the emcee for lots of gatherings, had a drink when I wanted it.

Well, I came home that summer. June, July ... by August I was packing. I couldn't wait to get back to the seminary.

Well, the years went by. Then it came time to be a deacon. I had been in the Serra Club, and they asked me to become a deacon at the first international convention. It was being held in London, across from Hyde Park in the Grosvenor House. Just a friend and I would be ordained. They had over a thousand Serrans there, a hundred priests, five bishops and a cardinal. I'll never forget it.

The fourth year went fast. Nothing to it. You were home free. The Pope decided that, during the Holy Year, those who wanted to could be ordained in Rome. Everyone else was ordained at the college in April, but I waited until July. I came out of the Pope's palace with 352 others and was ordained by Pope Paul VI at St. Peter's Basilica in the Square. There were a hundred thousand people there. It had never been done in Christianity before. About fifty people, family and friends, came from Minneapolis by charter to be with me.

I received a letter from the archbishop that I would be assigned to St. Leo's in Highland Village in St. Paul. It's a great parish. I suppose about twelve or fifteen hundred families. Just two of us priests. I was there about two and a half years, and then they needed somebody over at Maternity of Mary. That's in St. Paul, too, over by the cathedral. Then they asked me to come out here to Forest Lake and help, with the idea that maybe they'd give me a pastorate soon. So I came out here in June of 1978.

You know, I feel like I've been a priest all my life. I forget to mention sometimes that I have children. I'll say, well, I know because my boy ... or something like that, and their eyes will get big. I just assume that they know it.

One time I had gone out to dinner with a couple of priests, and on the way back I got into the wrong exit lane and got back into traffic. Well, way back were two flashing lights. The patrolman pulled me over and said: "Good evening, Father. Where are you going?" I said I was going to see my daughter. "Your daughter?" Then he asked to see my license. "Is this your address?" And I said no, that it was my son's. "Your son?" He said. "Do you mind stepping back here?" He figured he had a real live one now. "Tell me, Father," he said, "how much have you had to drink?" So I told him the whole story about my wife dying and my studies for the priesthood. He gave me a ticket.

Generally, the kids thought it was great when I told them I was going into the seminary. They knew that we could still be close. And we still are. My kids call me — they always call me — but they never lean on me. Take Mark, the youngest. He's with Western Airlines and flies out of here. Well, he called last night and said he's got a proposition — he's always got a proposition. He wants to buy the house that he's living in, and he wants to see where he can fit me into that picture. And I just may go along with him because it isn't a bad investment.

Some people come up and say that with all the experience I've had, I've got the answers. Well, I say: "Let me first clear you up; I don't have all the answers. But I know a lot of things that *don't* work." People come in and I'm not sure what the problem is, but I can spot easily where they're on the wrong track. So we try to get off of that and onto something else.

I don't think I know any more than other priests, but I think parishioners might have more confidence in me because they know I was married. They relate a little more easily.

When I was selling, after taking an order, a lot of times people would want to talk about their problems with me. They'd call their wife down and we'd talk about it. I was operating without a license, I guess. One guy said, "Well, you can be a priest, but I'm not going to confession to you." I said, "Come off of it.

You've been going to confession to me for twenty years!" You know, he'd been telling me everything all that time.

I use some of the old salesman talents, sure. You know how to present yourself. I think I'm selling the Catholic religion. I think I can show them the benefits of being a Catholic as opposed to some other brand. When I run up against the Jesus people, the Jesus freaks, the Moonies, all those other people, I just point to our track record: two thousand years is pretty good. And you know, being in the competitive business, it gives you a little motivation and aggressiveness for the work of God. I can't let any of them get ahead of me and my new company. You know the five great rules of a salesman: you get their attention, you hold their interest, you convince them the product is something they ought to have, you create the desire, and then you ask for the order. Well, you're doing that all the time when you sell Christ to others.

One of the biggest fears I had when I went to the seminary was that I'd lose interest, and sometimes I have that fear yet. I can't think of anything worse than not having the interest but having to answer to it. It would be terrible, like living in one place and wishing you were in another.

But I'm still excited about it. I find myself getting up at night because I've got an idea for a sermon. I get the same kind of feeling that I had when I called on a prospect and he said he'd give me an order. I hope I never lose it. Maybe when you get older, you do. I don't know.

I could have retired. I went in the seminary at fifty-six. Could have gone on in the company for another six years. And I wouldn't have had to work because I had everything set up. But I see too much of it — sixty-two, sixty-five, seventy: they're sitting there and puffin' and watching TV. You can get by with some of that, but I think you have to be doing something. No matter how old you are, there has to be something in each day toward the betterment of self in this pilgrimage toward God. There's got to be some feeling that you are making progress toward the ultimate goal. When you lose this, you start going down. I don't think you can stand still.

THOMAS SEGERSON

An Ordinary Guy

"God, I love this priesthood so much! Sometimes I look back and think maybe I wasted all those years. But then again I say, no, I got so much out of it. I find myself... when I'm hearing confessions and they get all through, I'll say something like, 'Golly, that sounds just like me.' "

By his own admission, Thomas Segerson is an ordinary guy. He likes to golf, go out to dinner, have a beer, be with friends. When a water pipe breaks, he fixes it; when something needs painting, he paints it. He gets angry if the phone rings a lot, but he gets over it.

Segerson is also a priest. He loves it. Once, when a former priest publicly described his disappointments, Segerson wrote a widely circulated article saying that, for himself, he was "totally, perfectly and even ridiculously happy." He likes what he can do for other people but admits, too, that he loves the priestly life-style.

At fifty-one, Segerson has been a priest only nine years. Before that he put out publications for various firms and was briefly news director for a small radio station. Most of his life has been spent in Madison, Wisconsin, where he is now an associate pastor of Immaculate Heart of Mary Church...

When a guy my age finally becomes a priest, people may think he spent nights and days in prayer, in church and everything. Well, I didn't that much. The priesthood was just an idea I had. It kept coming back. I do remember saying something like: "God, you've been bugging me long enough; if you want me, you can have me."

Always, way back in my mind, was that idea — ever since I was a little kid. But it would go away, and it wasn't very strong for a long, long time.

When I look back on it, I guess … I was going to say it was a period of searching, but I'm not so sure that it was. I was a day-to-day person. Whatever happens today, fine. I just floated around, really, from the time I got out of high school.

I went in the navy right out of high school in 1944. Most of the time I spent working in naval hospitals. I wanted to be a dentist at one time. That's why I enlisted in the hospital corps. But I got the lowest grade in chemistry in the history of the hospital corps, I think. I got a final grade of eighteen! Math and science — I liked them but I just couldn't get them. I decided then, "Well, that's it." I was in the navy a total of three and a half years and got out just before Christmas in '47.

Like a lot of guys, I didn't know for sure just what I wanted to do. I took a job in a factory here in Madison that made plastic seals for whisky bottles. I ran a printing press and looked at SEAGRAMS 7 CROWN for days and days and days. In the spring it got pretty hot and stuffy in there, so I wanted some outside work and went to work for a railroad on a section crew. One day a friend and I were talking, and he said, "Let's take advantage of the GI bill." So I applied at St. Thomas College in St. Paul and was accepted. I thought, "Well, I'll try this for a while."

I futzed around there for a while and finally got into English. And then the thought came, "I like to write; why not journalism?" They didn't have a journalism school, so after two years; I transferred to Wisconsin and graduated in '52.

I had decided in college that I would go into industrial journalism. My first job was with US Rubber in Joliet, Illinois. We put out a magazine every two weeks. Well, one day a professor

from school called and said there was a job with General Telephone Company in Madison, Wisconsin. So I came up and inter-
viewed and got that job. They had a magazine, a twenty-page
monthly, so I worked there for a while. I was getting as far as I
could go moneywise. They wanted me to give it up and join the
commercial department. In other words, eventually become a
manager of a local telephone office. But I wasn't too much for
that.

Now, Dad at this time was involved in a paper box company
in Wausau with some other guys. They were always after me to
sell; they thought I would make a good salesman. So when things
got kind of funny at the telephone company, I said, "Well, let's
look at that."

After a training session, they sent me up to Minneapolis to
sell boxes. I didn't sell boxes worth a damn. I was terrible. In the
first place, I was in Minneapolis, where there were all kinds of
box companies — and I was from one over in Wisconsin. I knew
the box business, how to design a package for a customer, but I
didn't know the ins and outs, the tricks of selling. They didn't
teach me any of those. A guy would say, "How many fives can
you give me?" — that means how much of a discount — and I'd sit
there and say, "Well, I'll have to call the office."

It was a bad time for me. I'd get up in the morning and go
off to my list of places to call on, walk in, and after two or three
nos, the day was just shot. I spent days just driving around in
my car. They finally realized I wasn't making much money for
them and called me back, and I went into the sales service department.

When I was in Minneapolis, I had met the vocations director
of the Dominican Fathers and talked to him about the priesthood.
When I was living in Wausau, I got kind of disgruntled and frustrated, and I decided to give it a try. I didn't talk to anybody
about it — my parents or anyone — but I went down and visited
the novitiate in Winona, Minnesota. One day I got a letter from
Father Graham, the vocations director. He said I should go down
to Loras College in Dubuque, Iowa, in September, and take some
Latin and philosophy courses first. I didn't want to do that. I

wanted to go right smack into the novitiate and really get this thing going. So I wrote back and said I thought I was going to change my mind.

One night I was sitting at a bar, having a drink in a hotel in Wausau, and this guy from General Telephone came up and said there was an opening at General Telephone again. So I went back in. By this time the company had expanded, and I was in the public relations department, editing the newspaper. I really enjoyed it.

Then I joined the Knights of Columbus here in Madison. With my background, they asked me to put out the state newsletter. The state deputy then was a guy from Platteville who owned a radio station. He asked me one day if I ever thought of going into radio. Well, he offered me more money than the telephone company was paying and said I would be news director. So I went to the telephone company and said, "Sorry, folks, I've tried it again and I'm going somewhere else."

This was 1960; I was thirty-four. I was the whole news department at Platteville. I'd go to the city council meetings, go out to fires and accidents and other things that happened. Most of our news came off the wire. There wasn't that much that really happened in that little town. It had less than ten thousand people. One big thing happened when the Thirty-second Division came home from Fort Lewis, Washington, and CBS made a big thing of that. CBS came to Platteville and covered it. Charles Collingwood came, and I remember interviewing him, sitting on a bench in front of the college. That was the neatest thing.

Well, money got tight, and the boss called me and a salesman in and said he was sorry but he just couldn't keep us on. That area just didn't have the business to bring in the advertising revenue. But we parted the best of friends and I still see him. I am glad to say business has improved and he has become quite successful.

I was unemployed for quite a while, finally landing a job with a developer here in Madison. His big thing is making prefabricated doctors' offices and he wanted me to edit a real fancy, arty magazine for the architecture people. I didn't want to go to work for him but he kept saying I was the guy he wanted. I didn't think I knew that much about that business, and he was never really that clear about exactly what he wanted me to do. All I ended up doing was a lot of photography. When a new doctor's office opened up, I'd go off for the opening and take pictures. He'd say "Fine!" and they'd end up in his scrapbook. There were days I'd sit at my desk and do absolutely nothing because everything I did had to be approved by him and he'd be off in Africa or somewhere. Finally one guy told me I was going to be fired. I thought I'd better quit before he fired me. So I quit.

And that's when I really began to do some soul-searching. All this futzing around from one job to another, never really completely satisfied, full of enthusiasm at first but then bored by the routine or not really doing anything. And I'd remained single. If I had a wife and kids, I would have stuck with something. All of a sudden the old idea about the religious life came back to me. So I went to see Father Graham of the Dominicans again. And we talked and talked and, all of a sudden, it hit me. I said, "It sounds to me like you're saying be a priest but the Dominicans don't want me." He said: "Well, it's not that we don't want you; but after you're in the seminary for a while, maybe you won't want us. You're too old (I was thirty-six). You're going to be with a lot of young kids, and they're going to find studying easier. It's going to be difficult for you in the novitiate with all these young kids."

So I went back and talked to my bishop, Bishop O'Connor. He said they'd give me a chance. So I looked up the file on seminaries and saw this listing for a place that accepted older men — Holy Apostles in Connecticut.

Then I finally told my parents. My mother didn't say that much, except that she was pleased that maybe I was going to find something in life. Dad's first remark was, "Why the hell didn't you do this ten years ago?"

Dad was ... well, Dad and I used to argue, mainly about money. Dad lost his job in the Depression, lost a lot of money, lost a two-story flat we had on the east side of Madison ... out of work a couple of years. I remember him doing landscaping for some doctor to pay for an ear operation I had to have. Dad always was telling me to save money. He'd write long letters when I was in the navy. Full of information. And there'd always be a paragraph in there about how I wasn't saving any money and how I'd better start saving some. Well, I was having a twenty-five-dollar bond taken out of my pay every month. I remember one time I sat down and wrote: "If you want me to go to the USO and have some little old lady give me cookies and milk, I'll do that. But that's not what a sailor does. We go out and go to bars and spend our money." I did not mail that letter, though. I just never worried about money.

Dad died of cancer in '70. I was a priest by then and officiated at his funeral. I didn't cry when he died because I firmly believe he's in heaven. About six weeks later it hit me that he was gone, and I had a good cry.

There were 133 in my class when I went to Holy Apostles in the fall of '63, but the dropout rate was fantastic. There were about fifty of us left at the end of the first year. Only five or six of us were ready for theology at the end of two years of philosophy and Latin. Several others from my class stayed on for three more years to earn a college degree.

It was a typical seminary life, like seminary life was until a few years ago. We did all the work there, everything. Even digging up pipes. Every Saturday was workday, and our first free day was the first Sunday in October. We had Wednesday afternoons off to go into town and shop, but we weren't supposed to go in taverns. I went from Labor Day until that Sunday in October without a beer. I almost went out of my mind, but I finally got used to it. In fact, I weighed 215 pounds when I went there in September; by the time I came home for Christmas, I weighed 178. The food wasn't that good. Let's face it: we were poor. We had a little truck and a guy would go out every morning to the grocery stores to get day-old bread and day-old produce. They did buy fresh meat. There were days ... for breakfast we might have a piece of toast and some cheese. It was good for me.

I really did find God there. I prayed like I had never prayed before. You know, I didn't really know who God was until I got

104

into the seminary. Yeah, I knew God was the Creator and we were supposed to obey Him, love and serve Him in this world and be happy with Him in the next; but He wasn't anything very personal. God was God, the Church was the Church, and I went to Mass on Sunday and to confession once in a while. I wasn't that close to God. I was a little afraid of Him ... because that's the kind of God I grew up with. I never really realized that God loved me, or I never really thought about it. I stayed in the Church, though — except for that navy period, of course. When I got out, I hadn't seen the inside of a church for two and a half, maybe three years. When I got out, I went to church again — but only because I had to. I really needed that seminary life-style to find out, for lack of a better word, who the heck I was working for.

For theology, I went to Catholic University in Washington. Studying, like Father Graham told me, was difficult. I got good grades — I'm proud of that — but I had to work for them. Some guys could sit down and read a book and remember. Me, I had to read something two or three times. My books are full of underlinings and notes in the margins. When I finally passed my oral exams for my master's degree in theology, some of my classmates put up a sign on my door: TOM SEGERSON, LIVING PROOF THAT YOU CAN TEACH AN OLD DOG NEW TRICKS.

I was ordained a deacon in '68 and a priest in '69. And I was assigned to teach at Beloit Catholic High School. I didn't like that. I just got a letter assigning me, and I didn't know whether I could argue about that or not. So I said, "Okay, I'll do it." They said they wanted me to teach American Church history, something I didn't know that much about. So I packed my bags and went back out to Catholic U and spent two or three weeks in the library, reading books and working up a course. I learned a lot; I don't know whether the kids did. How do you teach history? My method was just blah, blah, blah. And I was teaching it to sophomores. After ten minutes their attention span was gone. I was never trained to be a teacher. Discipline? All I knew was to shout at them. Later, when we were called up to the personnel board to see how things were going, I said I would like to be transferred. So I was assigned to St. Thomas Aquinas Parish here in Madison and was there about two years. Then I came here to Immaculate Heart of Mary in the fall of '72.

I like being a priest, I thoroughly enjoy it. There are times, you know ... like any work, there are phases I don't particularly care for but that I'll do. I think particularly of counseling. I'm a lousy counselor. I have no training. The guys that are coming out of the seminary now — they have training. We didn't have any of that. I never had counseling before. When I counsel people, I'm very easily frustrated when I can't come up with an easy, quick answer. I guess I'm honest enough to admit that to them. I find myself — like in a marriage situation — taking sides. If the woman is the first one who comes and tells me all her problems, I'm immediately prejudiced against the guy before I even listen to him. I don't get as many people coming to me for counseling as the other priests do.

Other than that, I like being with people. I like little kids. Every child who gets ready for First Communion has to come and see me, and I have more fun with these kids. I like the older kids too. I don't get much chance to work with high-school kids. We have two Catholic schools they go to, and the public school kids have CCD in their homes. I like being with adults too.

I enjoy all the sacramental aspects too. One of my favorite days is Friday, when I bring Communion to the sick and the homebound. I don't just go in and, you know, light the candle and say the prayers. I stick around and talk to them. I tell the people I wouldn't do this if I didn't believe it was important.

I know people here kind of like it because I'm folksy. There's nothing churchy about me. You know some priests, when they come out of the sacristy door, they're entirely different: they're pontifical. Why is it that some priests are so different around the altar? I try not to be that way. I try to be just the way I am. If somebody ever tries to put me up on a pedestal, to make me something that I'm not ... well, I don't want that. If sometimes I'm obnoxious ... if I'm bombed or anything, I don't want people saying Father is sick, or Father is this or that. If anybody does that, well, in fact I told God, I'll leave. I have to be who I am.

I use the experience I had before ... yes. For example, a guy comes to me with a drinking problem. Some of the things he tells me that he's done, I've done. You know, like he's talking about how he sometimes drives home and wonders how he got home. Well, I've experienced that. I've done a lot of beer drinking in my day. That was my social life. There were times when I drove home with one eye closed so I only saw eight headlights on a car instead of sixteen. And I'd wonder ... you know ... how I did it. So I talk to him about it, and then I throw in something like I thank God for the fact that I didn't kill somebody.

I'm less mystical than a lot of priests. I don't pray as much as I should. I go in streaks. I don't read the Office every day. All during Advent, I never missed a day. Now it's sitting up on my table and getting dust on it. I haven't used it since Christmas. Eventually I'll pick it up again. I don't pray the rosary much, except at a wake. I guess I'm like a lot of people today — God will show up when I'm alone, outside. I remember touring the Alps one summer. I had some extra dough and time off. We were up on the top of Mont Blanc, and I was standing there and I blurted out to the guy next to me, "You know, you can't stand on a place like this and say there is no God." And he said he was thinking the same thing. Sometimes, God's really, really close.

My life-style hasn't changed that much. I still do the things I used to do. Years ago the vow of poverty always got to me. I'd say: "Well, gee, God, I want to be a priest, but I don't want to give up my golf clubs. I want to have money to spend." I didn't understand what the vow of poverty meant. I do a lot of things that I did before. I play golf, go bowling. Two weeks ago I had a ball. Our bowling team went out and spent the kitty from last year. We had drinks at this guy's house, then we went out to eat. And I was dancing — I hadn't danced in ten years. And I was doing the polka and everything!

My best friends are lay people. I tend to be drawn for social activities to lay people rather than to priests. Maybe that's wrong. My best friends are a man and his wife that I've known ever since I joined the Knights of Columbus. We try to have dinner together every Friday night. I've been on vacation with them. At the Priests' Senate meeting the other day, we got on the subject of vocations. From that we went to the fact that as priests we need to support one another. Then maybe people will see that we have a real camaraderie and will say they want to get into that. And one guy who had been out of the priesthood for about two years and then came back spoke up. "I'm not sure that's what I need," he said. "The people that I trust and need are lay people. They got me back into the priesthood." I told him later that my social life, too, revolves around lay people. I'm in a house where there are four priests. We eat together and we do things together, but I don't socialize with them. About the only time I look to another priest is when I want to play golf and all my lay friends are working. But even then I hesitate—they're probabiy busy.

Financially I'm better off now than when I was out of the priesthood. Before I went in, I didn't have any money, really. I didn't have a savings account. I had a huge debt on my car. Now I've got money in the bank and I've got an annuity program going so I'll have some money when I retire.

I don't think celibacy is a problem at all. I have a feeling I would have ended up a crummy old bachelor. Oh, I was engaged once. There was a girl in Chicago, but, you know, I never really proposed to her. It was New Year's Eve and I said, "What would happen if I asked you to marry me?" That was the wrong thing to say because that's all she heard: I was hooked. Well, it didn't last. She wasn't the one I really wanted to marry though. That was a girl at the university. She was a freshman and I really loved her. She was a lot younger than I. If I ever had gotten up the courage to ask her to marry me, I think I would have been the happiest guy in the world.

But celibacy? I agree that maybe there should be the option, maybe some guys can function better as married priests. But I think I can serve people better this way. If I were married and had a wife and children, would they suffer because of what I want to be as a priest? Would they come first or last? Suppose one of the children was very sick and I got a phone call and was needed somewhere else. Would I leave that poor sick kid there and go to that other person? I don't think I would.

I don't have a problem with loneliness. In this place and in the other places I've been, you don't have time to be lonely. Maybe if I get stuck in some little burg where the doorbell rings once a week, I might get lonesome. But I know that I can always find friends.

I relate to other priests differently ... because of age. See, I'm fifty-one. I could have been ordained maybe twenty-five years ago. I haven't gone to school with those guys and been assigned to parishes with them. Consequently, I know nothing of their past history; nor do they of mine. We don't have that much in common. But I think I'm accepted. I'm the president of the Priests' Senate now. I really didn't want that, but several guys came to me and said, "We want you."

I want to be a pastor, I really do — not to be a boss but to have my own place. I would like to get into a smaller place and really get to know all my parishioners. And I've been told that now they are not considering, so much, years in the priesthood as age and experience.

I am so happy being a priest. I think there are a lot of guys floating around out there who could have some of this happiness, this freedom, this closeness to God. When I first went into the seminary and a guy would leave, that would really bother me. It bothered me because from the day I walked into that place, I said to myself, "Segerson, you found a good thing; you've got it made." When I saw a guy leave, I'd think, "Dammit, he's cutting out; he's not going to be around to share this good thing." I made up my mind when I was ordained that no matter how angry or frustrated or irritated or sick or anything else I was, whenever I was in the presence of a young man, like an altar boy or someone, I would try to give him the idea that I was happy — even if I had to fake it. But I don't have to fake it. I really am happy.

PATRICK HIGGINS

A Searcher for Something More

"After I got out of the service and until I started seriously to pursue this religious vocation, I liked the things that I was doing very much. But none of them gave me a feeling of stability and a feeling of ... vocation. The social work, the urban planning, going to law school — it seemed like I was just working for myself, even though I found the jobs satisfying. And there seemed to be a message from God, down deep, that said, 'Pat, you're not supposed to be working for yourself.'

"It just seemed always that there was something more — more to be done, more to be considered. It was really not until I started thinking about the religious life that those questions and that 'more-ness' started to resolve."

At St. Martin of Tours Parish, in a battered area of the Bronx, Father Patrick Higgins puts down the homily he is preparing for tomorrow's Mass and talks to a visitor. It will be a Spanish Mass, and Higgins is just learning the language. His pastor will have to make some corrections.

Broad-shouldered, Irish, and with a thatch of brown hair, Higgins at thirty-four looks like a young John Kennedy, whose spirit of hope he respected; or like a football player, which he was in college. As a center and linebacker, he played on the Holy Cross team, but was "not quite big enough and definitely not fast enough" to do much else with it.

Like many college graduates, Higgins was not sure of his career and went from one job to another, then another. But, unlike many others, he worried about the lack of direction in his life. He began to read and to talk to others about his future. And then, as it has for many other priests, Thomas Merton's book The Seven Storey Mountain *provided a glimpse of what that future might be.*

Newly ordained, Higgins finds that his past job experience is helping him work with the mostly Hispanic and black community that makes up St. Martin of Tours Parish...

I knew I was involved in things that were helping other people, but there seemed to be some aspect of my life that was not filled. At the time, I had no real personal relationship with God. I had a faith and a certain structure in terms of virtue and values, but they weren't vital. They didn't energize my life.

And, as far as my work was concerned, I couldn't look down the road further than six months, a year, a year and a half.

Social work? Well, I was a caseworker up in Harlem for the New York Social Services Department. It was visiting homes, mostly apartments, and dealing with broken families, trying to maintain the income of families, and also trying to give some direction and support to people who were trying to make something of their lives and get off the welfare cycle. There was some limited success. But the syndrome of urban difficulties and poverty is so difficult to break out of that, in the long run, it came down to just maintaining the family's income.

In my case, as in most cases, the caseload was so overwhelming that I never had the opportunity to devote the time necessary to help a particular family. At one point I think I had seventy-five or eighty individuals or families to deal with. It was just impossible. We were supposed to visit every one each month. I was outrageously frustrated. Everyone was. There seemed not to be any great hope of breaking the welfare cycle.

Whether it became so totally overwhelming or whether I saw some greater opportunity, I transferred. This time it was a job in the city Housing and Development Administration. I worked as a project coordinator in the Model Cities program. As you remember, this was a remnant of the Kennedy-Johnson social legislation.

What we did there was liaison with community groups who were empowered to set their own course and who had a great input into what the governmental agencies were doing. We would spend quite a bit of time out in the field, meeting with community groups, visiting buildings that needed rehabilitation. There was quite a bit of personal involvement.

There were a lot of aspects to the Model Cities effort that I found attractive. It was in the late sixties, turning into the seventies, and there was a lot of vitality in the people involved. The upheaval of the sixties was still going on and was very real in New York. There was an awful lot of spirit. It was good work.

But the program was so new, so completely theoretical at this point, it was sometimes frustrating too. I wound up spending a year as assistant to the commissioner, who then left to take a job with a state agency. I didn't want to go along.

And I'd been thinking about law school for some time. It had always been presented to me as an excellent background for any kind of governmental or even business work. And my father was a lawyer in private practice.

My parents were second-generation Irish, and I come from a traditional Catholic family. Very much so. My five brothers, my sister, and I grew up on Long Island, and my parents were very insistent that we get a Catholic education. I know that I was reared in what I have come to understand as a typical Catholic environment of the late forties and fifties. Religion had a lot to do with what you did and did not do. But, at the same time, I think there was an awful lot of youthful mystery involved.

In school there was a lot of discipline, but there was also a lot of excellent education. In the last several years I've heard and read critics of Catholic education. Perhaps their religion was forced on them more than it was forced on me, because I don't recall it with any of the hostility or resentment that some of these people feel. That is not to say that I don't agree in principle with many of the things they're saying.

You know, the Church has changed so much since that time. If I had developed the way I have over the years and the Church had remained the structured, institutional, less-than-charismatic Church that existed then, I don't think I would find myself in this position today.

In grade school, being a priest was the only thing I wanted to do. But that sentiment stopped almost immediately in my first year of high school. You know ... social life, sports, girls take up all of our time and thoughts. If you saw the movie *American Graffiti*, that was just our high-school time. When I first saw that movie, I laughed my head off because, there it was, as plain as day up on the screen.

My father was very much interested in the Jesuit method of education. I went to Holy Cross College because of that direction — and the fact that Holy Cross had a football team. My college career began with a yearlong party, otherwise known as my freshman year. I was young, a year younger than most everyone else. I had skipped a year in grammar school, and I really hadn't made the psychological adjustment to the work that was necessary. And I spent all my time with the social life, athletics, and other things.

Things changed after my first year — mainly because I did so poorly that something had to be done. I had a good year my third year, academically, and then senior year continued the same way.

I'd been in the ROTC in college and, after graduation, I was commissioned as a second lieutenant in the Marine Corps and went through basic infantry officer training in Quantico, Virginia. After that, I went to the Naval Air Training Command at Pensacola, Florida, to train as a pilot.

The military was something that ... well, I don't know if it was a heartfelt choice. My father had been in the Marine Corps. I was happy to be in the service. It was the normal thing to do at the time. That time, 1965, was when the activity in Vietnam was just beginning to escalate seriously. When I started, none of us knew anything about war or the prospect of it. Vietnam was a place thousands of miles away. By the time it became a reality — you know, our next assignment — it was different. Guys who had trained with us at Quantico were writing back, and we knew guys who had been killed, shot, maimed. That put a whole new perspective in our lives.

Since we were still in flight training, war was not too imminent. It was not a constant topic of conversation or cause of anxiety, but it was something that started to grow and grow in our minds.

I had hurt my leg in a football game in college my last year. Then I played for a team in Pensacola and I hurt it again. I tore the knee ligaments in college; they were never repaired, and the knee was weak. So the naval physicians recommended that I be discharged as not physically qualified. To be honest, that was fine with me. While I enjoyed being in the service, it was very clear to me that the military had no long-term interest for me. There were a lot of aspects of it — its discipline and posturing — that I really didn't agree with.

I was not too much aware of who I was and what I was doing at that time. I was maturing, but very slowly. Politically, socially, sexually, psychologically — I don't think that I was too terribly aware of who I was. I was only twenty or twenty-one at that time. It was all beginning: the gears were really just starting to turn.

I was very, very malleable. I remember how strongly I felt, but how totally helpless I was. When I think about that period, I remember it so clearly that I really hope it helps me to deal with and relate to people of that age in my work as a priest. And as a counselor, as a friend.

My active church life had waned seriously around the middle of college. Some theological questions came up that were not satisfactorily answered by the *pro forma* theological and philosophical education I was offered in this traditional Catholic school. I didn't pursue the answers all that intensely, but it was clear to me that the ones offered were not satisfactory. So my sacramental and church life took a nosedive that lasted through

114

the service. But my church life never completely disappeared. I went to Mass because it was a good thing to do ... once a month or every couple of weeks. And I remember going to a chaplain at Pensacola and making a general confession. So I was trying to maintain some degree of spiritual life.

When I got out, I really started to read, and serious life questions began to become a real concern for me. The questions became greater, more real, more serious, more anxious; but also more fun and more honest. I'm sure everyone has grand hopes of finding great answers to these questions; but until I started thinking about the religious life, I can't recall coming up with any ... you know ... biggies.

So, after I got out of the service, which was February of '67, I really had made no vocation decision. My first job was with the Chase Manhattan Bank in an executive training program. I liked the job a great deal, but I felt strongly that it wasn't what I wanted seriously for a future. I had odd jobs for a while before I answered an advertisement in one of the New York papers for the social services job. Then there was the Model Cities job, and then I entered Fordham Law School.

As I said, there was a real lack of stability and a lack of direction in my life. I started doing more reading so that I wouldn't be totally immersed in the law books and studies. And after so many years, the idea of the priesthood came about pretty suddenly and directly. It was a certain section of Thomas Merton's *Seven Storey Mountain*.

Reading that passage from that book, I find it hard to describe exactly what happened. It was just a short paragraph or two—I don't even recall the exact passage or what it said. It had something to do with the absurdity of vanity.

Those couple of paragraphs were the real key for me. Well, the best way I can describe it is that it coalesced or crystallized or ... whatever ... all of the divergent philosophical and theological concerns that I had at that time. Somehow it put my innermost thoughts into some sort of perspective and forced me to step out of my small, personal shell and look at the universe differently. It planted a seed in my mind which never left and kept growing. It became something that I obviously had to devote some time and attention to. I knew I had to consider the religious life.

During that whole year in law school, I was dating a young woman very seriously. We were in love, and we were at the point where we would have to seriously consider marriage. That was something very obvious to us. I was very close to her, and she was absolutely lovely.

But during that time, all these other thoughts kept getting stronger and stronger. I did not do well that year in law school, so I would not have been able to go right back to school the next September. In October I made a retreat at a monastery to try to figure out exactly what was going on and how strongly this spiritual calling seemed to be. I came from the retreat and had a very pleasant reunion with my girl friend. But I knew that this was going to need a lot more attention.

That continued and we decided that we would have to be separated for some time and see how things developed. So I didn't see her for the next few months, and that was ... well, difficult. But it became more and more clear that my direction was more toward the spiritual life. I wasn't sure what it was specifically about the priesthood or a religious vocation at the time, but I was more and more sure that my relationship with this young woman was not in the future. That was hard.

I was living in Manhattan at the time, by myself, in a very cheap studio-type apartment on East Ninety-fifth Street, working odd jobs as a bartender and occasionally as a taxicab driver. Both gave me flexibility to seek some spiritual counseling and vocational direction. So I saw a priest, a Dominican priest, at St. Catherine of Siena Church on Manhattan's East Side. His sermons had influenced me, and I had gone to that church regularly because the girl lived right around the corner. I had been trying very seriously to get the practice of my faith and religion back in shape after many years of being lax.

So I spoke to Father Connolly regularly, every couple of weeks or so. Merton's book influenced me a lot toward consideration of the monastic life, and I also had some feeling toward missionary activity. But I still wasn't certain.

I heard about a group known as the Little Brothers of Jesus, located in Detroit. It was attractive. Their way of life seemed to be a combination of the monastic way and missionary activity. They considered themselves contemplatives, yet they work in the middle of normal but poor conditions.

Their way is to accept visitors and aspirants and allow them to live there for six months to a year to test their calling for that particular way of life. So, after clearing up my affairs in New York, paying my debts, and vacating my apartment, that's what I did. I took a job with one of the other men in the house and just lived with them and accepted their way.

When I left for Detroit, it had become clear to me that this was what I wanted to do, that it was my life's work and direction. But also that it was what God wanted me to do. And, from that time on, I really haven't had any doubts about the priesthood. There haven't been any times when I seriously questioned again what my direction or what God's plan for my life was.

One of the aspects of the Brothers' way of life is that each week they spend at least an hour in talking over the past week: how life has gone, personal emotions, feelings, tensions, concerns, aspirations. It was called a "review of life," and as we talked about my own life, I found that very helpful. But I still wasn't sure whether their way of life was what I was interested in. I felt then and I do now, though, that their way and their vision have had a profound influence on my "formation."

The diocesan priesthood at first had not been an interest of mine, but as time went by it seemed to grow stronger and stronger. While I was in Detroit, I heard about Pope John Seminary. There were several things that attracted me to it — mainly the aspect of their consideration of older men.

Well, I made an application to Pope John while I was in Detroit. They accepted me, and I went there in the fall of '74. Since I was from New York, the archdiocese here wanted me to transfer to their seminary, Dunwoodie, after a year; but I was so happy at Pope John that I didn't want to. I spent three years there, transferred to Dunwoodie my final semester, and completed my academics and my deacon year with my class there.

Two of the summers during the seminary, I spent right here at St. Martin of Tours; so I was delighted when I was assigned here after ordination. I was familiar with the people, the teachers, many of the children from the day camp that I ran and other parish work I had done. It was exactly the type of parish that I wanted to come to.

I'm just starting to learn the language—and that's a challenge—but I don't feel a difficult cultural or ethnic lack. I think people are people, no matter where they're from, and their needs are the same.

You know, my experiences in the past have shown me that while cultural differences are real, they are in many cases exaggerated into barriers. And since the work we're involved in is of a transcendental nature, I choose to disregard them. If I were coming into this without my previous experiences, in a neighborhood such as this — culturally and ethnically different — I might not feel the same way. I might feel very threatened or very nervous, but I don't. And I'm old enough now too. If I were twenty-four instead of thirty-four in this kind of assignment, I would feel a lot different than I do now.

Mainly, I feel the truth of my relationship with God so deeply and so honestly — the difference that it's made in my life — that I really want to tell people about it. I want them to understand, and I want them to agree with me, to live their lives that way too. It's a constant challenge and, consequently, a constant frustration.

Sometimes it's responded to; most of the time it's not — at least not in the way I'd like it to be. You say something to somebody and you want them to say, "Yeah, I really understand." Well, that's not the way it goes. But the satisfactions, when they arise, are so great, so grand and glorious, that they provide the sustenance and support that you need.

And there are also ambitions, loads of hopes and dreams, glorious undertakings that keep you going.

I'm very contented and happy. There isn't anything missing from my life that I feel strongly now. I know that I have a lot of work to do, a lot of growing to do spiritually, personally, psychologically, and every other way to be better at what I do. But I do not feel there is anything essential missing.

Sex... I don't find that overwhelmingly difficult. Recollections of relationships that were physical in the past certainly intrude into my life now, and the fact that they might exist now is attractive. It's very real, a very real concern and question, but it doesn't seem to be overpowering or cause me any serious distracting difficulties.

I have some close relationships with women. I like women a lot and like to be around them a lot. I really enjoy the natural chemistry that exists. But I've never felt that I've been playing games with reality. It's something that's very real. I discuss it with my friends who are priests and celibates fairly often, and I discuss it with women. It was not something that I thought an awful lot about when I made the decision for priesthood. I don't think I'm repressing or sublimating or anything like that, but the idea of not having sexual intercourse for the immediate future or even the long term was not something that had a big part to play in my choice of a life that involved celibacy.

I'm concerned about optional celibacy ... for those who are concerned about it. I would like it to be a matter of choice because I don't think it's right for everybody. I'm not sure what my choice would be. At this point it's not a question for me. I think my life as a priest, as a person for God, right now ... well, I'm not positively sure, but I think that celibacy is right for me.

The reason I wanted to be a priest is that I feel I have a real, honest, and, I hope, growing relationship with God ... a personal relationship. I feel that God is in my life now, very truly, very deeply, very tangibly, and with a force and a power that is not really able to be resisted. And I don't have any desire to resist it. I want to relate to God with my whole person and my whole life.

It's obvious that anyone can do this in a million different ways, but I don't think I could do this without being a priest. This is for me and for right now. I don't know about the future — but I don't think about that very much. I picture myself growing older and maturing, growing in my vocation and my spiritual life, in my personal life, in my relationship with God.

119

At the moment, I don't think there is any way I could build up this relationship better or even as well as I'm able to do it as a priest. I honestly believe that this is the way God wants me to live my life.

My mother once asked my why I wanted to be a priest. Well, in fact, what I want to do is be a good man, a good Christian man. That's what I really want to do. Being a priest is only the mode, the way in which I do that. But underneath it all, I just want to try to be a good man for God.

GEORGE KLEPEC

A Lawyer in Social Service

"What attracted me to the priesthood was the element of service. No question about it. There was some of that present in my law practice and in my other activities, too, in my ten years before entering. But priesthood to me means ministry and serving the people. *Service* is the main word: service within the context of Christian teaching, which is the Gospel."

Father George Klepec bounds up the stairs of the old brick building, a converted house, and points out the rooms where exciting things are happening. This is the Dr. Martin Luther King Adult-Education Center in Kankakee, Illinois, a place that helps a wide variety of people get a new start in their careers.

As president of the center's board of directors, "Father George," as he likes to be called, does administrative work, fund raising, promotion, problem solving, and a variety of other chores he dismisses under the heading of "things like that." Besides the education programs, the center has a day-care facility, a nursery, and projects for others, young and old.

It's one of several hats Klepec wears. He's also a member of the board of directors and secretary of a drug rehabilitation center in Kan-

kakee, and director of the Campaign for Human Development in the Joliet diocese. He is associate pastor of St. Stanislaus Church, a small parish that attracts people from throughout the community because of its liturgy, its warmth, and the social concerns it expresses.

Klepec seems to have boundless energy, but he's also a cool professional. As the lawyer he was (and is), he seems to approach life case by case, issue by issue. He regards the priesthood as a profession because "it's service-oriented, people-oriented." He has switched from one profession to another, and his direction seems secure...

During my diaconate, I worked one summer with Father Joe Burns, who did a lot of work with migrants and poor blacks, and he asked me if I was interested in doing social action work. I told him I definitely was interested. I'd been involved in social work before, so it was planned that after about three or four years I would replace the fellow who was here.

Since I came here in '75, the social action has been building on what has been. In other words, I saw my role as improving the programs that already existed, sharpening them up the best I could, because they are excellent programs and they serve the community well.

It's a lot different from the sixties; we don't have confrontations anymore, and there's building within the system. I've always felt that I could work within the system, that I could be a bridge between the system and the nonsystem. It seems I've always felt comfortable in a wide variety of situations. With minority groups, for example. I was raised in a neighborhood that was changing, and I never felt out of place. So that has always been easy for me, though I know it is a matter of culture shock for some guys.

The King Center is in the middle of a black neighborhood, but it has a lot of white participation, some of which has been long-standing. When you go there, you'll find that a third to a half of the students are white because the people of Kankakee have found that if you want good preparation for your GED tests, that's the place to go.

The people who come here are mostly adults who have a

strong motivation to better themselves, either because of job opportunities or a change in their life status. When their kids have grown up, for example. A more typical example would be young men and women who drop out of high school and, after they get to be twenty-four or twenty-five and have never been able to get a decent job, finally come to grips with the fact that they are educationally deprived. Sister Marianne, who is the principal of the center, sits them down and gives them tests to determine what level they're reading at and what level of math skills they have. For some people it's a milestone to get to the seventh- or eighth-grade level: it's a tremendous difference from where they were when they came in.

We do a lot of other community functions too. During the Thanksgiving and Christmas seasons we're involved in such things as Christmas baskets and toys, kids' parties and games. We have blood pressure testing, bring in the bloodmobile — that sort of thing. In the summer we run a two- or three-week basketball clinic, and as many as a hundred kids turn out. I've always played ball myself and keep a close interest in organized sports, especially basketball. I keep in good physical condition and still get into games occasionally.

At the drug rehabilitation center, we've changed from a more relaxed setting, where the dominant personalities were former drug users, to a more clinical-type setting, where the prominent personalities are professional people. It's right on the main street, in the walk-in area, and it's been an outstanding thing for this community. Our methadone clientele is about forty-five, with about seventy-five more in psychological counseling and group counseling.

Another of my concerns is a group of Mexican families who have settled about seven or eight miles outside of Kankakee and work in the fields there. They have a lot of children and, through the King Center, we've had bilingual programs for them and second-language classes for the adults. During the winter, a lot of them are in Texas or Mexico, visiting their relatives. When they get back, I go and check everybody out, see who's around, who has to be baptized, and what else is happening. This is pastoral work.

I'm convinced that the Church has to be involved in this sort of thing. If it's going to preach a Christian witness, it has to give a Christian witness. If it preaches a Gospel for all mankind, that means it preaches equality. If it simply catered to the wealthy class, or the working class, it would eliminate efforts in relation to the poor. It just wouldn't be giving witness to the Gospel of Christ. I think the Church has always been willing to have people working among the poor; it's one of the highest forms of witness. I think of St. Vincent de Paul in this regard, just to name one.

As for my taking part ... well, I think everybody recognizes there's definitely a place for concerned clergy. You almost have to ask, "Why not?" You can't close out an interested person, just because he's a clergyman, from dealing in activities where human interests are involved. In an area like day care, for example, there is an intensive human interest that is very attractive to the clergy. Or take young people at the drug center — potentially serious social problems. That very much attracts a person who is grooved into the Gospel. The average parish deals with these problems on a more local and specific level; I'm just doing them on a community level.

You get a tremendous amount of satisfaction from doing this. I'm not always successful, and I'm not always good at it. Things don't always work out as you think they should, but you just keep going at it. I consider myself adaptable, which is a strong point that I have. In the two previous places I worked, I did a lot of jail visitation, and I did youth work on a community level rather than just on a parish level. So I've had a broader scope.

Now, all of what I'm saying here must be understood in the context of my priestly vocation. The Holy Spirit plays the most important part of all in these things, needless to say. You have to recognize His presence and influence at all times — if you're going to keep your feet on the ground. And, of course, there's the necessary element of personal spirituality. That's got to be said constantly. Without that, you risk slipping out of your vocation. I'm afraid that might have happened to a lot of those who left the priesthood in recent years.

This is my third assignment. I was at St. Michael's in

Wheaton for about four years, and then at St. Pat's in Joliet for a year and a half. I really enjoyed that year and a half, being in my hometown, though that wasn't my home parish. I knew a lot of people there. I've still got warm feelings for both those places. This one too.

Joliet is a very Catholic town. When I was a kid, it was sixty to sixty-five percent Catholic, which they said was second only to Providence, Rhode Island. Now it's probably fifty percent. So I was raised in a very Catholic atmosphere, and you never felt that you were the minority. It wasn't until I studied about it later that I realized there are places in this country where there are very few Catholics, and sometimes bias is shown against them.

Ours was a traditional ethnic Catholic family. My father came here from Slovenia in northern Yugoslavia, but by the time I came on the scene our family was pretty thoroughly Americanized. My dad was in a variety of things. He sold insurance and involved himself with real estate; he was a Democratic politician and justice of the peace for eight years during the Depression era. He was involved in Slovenian fraternal organizations and was editor of a Slovenian-American newspaper.

I don't think I missed a Sunday Mass in my life. Well, maybe when I was sick once or twice when I was a kid. I remember when I was in basic training, down in Fort Leonard Wood, I was the only guy, in my barracks anyway, who'd get up at seven-thirty on Sunday mornings, get dressed, and go to church. Everybody else was sacked out. Later, a couple of guys did come with me after I assured them it was worth their while. But that's when I realized how I was raised. It was just so automatic for me to get up and go to church that I never gave it a second thought. I didn't care if everybody else slept in. If they wanted to, that was their choice.

My dad died when I was in grade school, and my mom died when I was a high-school freshman. The rest of us stayed together — my brother and four sisters, all older than I. The next youngest is seven years older than I, and the oldest is twenty years older; so we have a broad spectrum of ages. Also, one of my sisters, Sister Elizabeth Marie, has been a Franciscan for thirty years. I give my brother and my sisters a lot of credit for always treating me like an equal. I wasn't the little kid; I was one of the brothers and sisters — and that was important to me.

My freshman year of high school was pretty rough because of Mom's serious illness, and I remember I was involved with Mass on a daily basis. I remember at the end of that school year, after my mother's death, one of the Carmelite priests at Catholic High asked me if I thought I might have a vocation to the priesthood. That surprised me because I had never thought of it at all. I told him right out: "Not really." But from that time on, until the end of high school, it was probably always in the back of my mind. Not seriously, though, because I was looking toward the law as a career and had no real thoughts of the priesthood.

By the time I graduated from high school, I knew that I would be a lawyer. My brother, Joe, is a lawyer, and Dad had been a justice of the peace, as I've said. Also, the romance of the legal profession attracts you to some extent. But mostly I think it was just a case of a young man realizing that he had to pick a profession. I was in a college-prep school, and you know how everybody is *pre*-this or *pre*-that. So it wasn't at all hard for me to choose prelaw, and I did.

First I went to Joliet Junior College, then to Lewis University, and then to DePaul University in Chicago for the law degree. Through all this, there wasn't time to think about the priesthood because I was too deeply involved in my studies. I mean, you live like a monk during the school year. You work all the time. I was living at home all those years and commuting the forty miles back and forth every day. I'd get on the train at seven-thirty in Joliet, study on the train, go to school, do a lot of library work in the afternoon. When I got home at six, I'd be whipped, but I'd still always have some cases to brief. My main recreation in those days was playing some bridge on weekends.

After law school, I went into the Army Reserves because there was that military obligation. I was so relieved to be out of school and to have passed the bar exam and not to have to think for the next six months of active military duty. That's true. They just take your brain away from you. Luckily, this was right in between Berlin and Vietnam: the thing in Berlin had calmed down and the war in Vietnam hadn't heated up yet.

During those months that I was in Army training, I was almost always a little older than everybody else in my group. And during this time, a lot of guys were seeking me out, guys who had problems. Part of it was that they knew I was a lawyer, but part of it was that I am naturally a moderate person. I mean I was a nondrinker (still am), and I suppose it was obvious to the guys that I wasn't a goof-off or a clown. I guess they were just looking for someone who was basically stable that they could talk to ... about a lot of things — the girl back home, their family, the sergeant, discipline, routine, trying to put their life together.

This wasn't new. Although my interest in people and their problems came out most broadly during the time I spent with the law firm, I would have to say that even way back as a kid in grade school I always wound up trying to make life easier for kids who were having a hard time, either tutoring or befriending kids who had problems. I didn't realize that until I reflected on it years later, but I guess it was always part of my life.

So it was really during the service that I started giving some thought to the priesthood. It was just that these guys were coming to me with their problems, and I knew I was helping them. Then when I got out of active duty, I joined a law firm in Joliet. I was the youngest of six lawyers, and as a young lawyer you wind up doing a lot of domestic relations cases. One of the reasons is you sit close to the door, and the women — in those days more women than men would come in — would not be looking for any particular lawyer, so the young guys would wind up with those cases.

The cases were eye-opening for me. It was just a case of a young man suddenly entering the real world. It was not that I didn't have a realistic outlook — I think I did — but it was the first time that I was so personally and so very deeply involved in the lives of other people. I was able to see human problems in greater depth, really becoming a part of these problems, and yet being detached enough to work on them. Looking back, I'm amazed to some extent. There I was, a twenty-five-year-old kid, green — oh, how green I was! — and people would come in and put their whole lives out there on the table. I used to think to myself: if I were they, I wouldn't want to say those things to me. I was just happy that I had enough savvy to deal with it. I think it was because I had so many years of self-confidence built up in me. I belonged to a stable family, and I knew I was always loved and accepted. I just didn't have to worry about those things.

The law practice was a good one all the way around. The firm was all Catholic, and they were very strong on high ideals and helping people. It wasn't just a case of making a dollar. We did a lot of work for free. That was their way of doing business, and I've always admired them for it. They were more interested in seeing that the lawyers did a good job for the clients than in piling up a lot of money. I really appreciated that.

The first year I made around ten thousand dollars, and that was back in '63, when starting salaries in a small town were like six or seven thousand. So that was a pleasant surprise. And I was making about fifteen thousand by the time I left a few years later. I was advancing and I was pleased with that.

I started thinking about the priesthood more and more during the law practice. Every summer I'd go to the Army Reserve summer camp, and just about every time, I'd seek out the chaplain and have a talk with him about the possibility of priesthood. I was involved in religious things — CCD, Bible-study groups — things like that. And I was going to daily Mass (I found a Mass in the late afternoon that was just ideal for me), which gave me a further stability factor I needed. Just a trust and confidence in the Lord. Not that there were going to be any miracles but that, no matter what came up, we'd be able to work it out.

So, you see, God was always a part of my life. When a religious vocation came into the picture, it seemed to agree with the idea that God was part of my life.

It was about then that I got to thinking that the priesthood and my personality were compatible. Not that the law practice and my personality were incompatible, but suddenly I was seeing possibilities that I had never seen before.

As I said before, I was able to see the kinds of service that priests could give to people. It was the greater involvement with people that attracted me. I'd always been interested in that and had close contact with people from the time I was growing up. Now there seemed to be an opportunity to do more. In my law practice I felt that I was able to relate professionally to maybe one, two, three people at the most at any one time. I think I really felt the need to relate to more people.

And then, of course, those were the years of renewal in the Church, so there definitely was an excitement about it. Identifying with the Church at that time was something good. You felt you wanted to be a part of it. It was a lively atmosphere, for sure.

So, putting all of this together, I did feel a call. It wasn't anything like a bolt of lightning. It was much more gradual, just like most things in my life have been. And when I finally made a move in the direction of the priesthood, it all started to roll. Things just kind of fell into place.

So I sought out the young priest at St. Joseph's, my home parish. He was a late vocation himself — in fact, he was a lawyer — and I told him about it, and he told me about Pope John Seminary in Boston. I was surprised about that. If he had said, "Well, you have to go to St. Such and Such, and you'll be going with twenty-one-year-olds," I don't know how I would have responded. But there was this place for late vocations. Wow! And as it turned out, it made my seminary life much easier.

I think Pope John Seminary is excellent for training men for the priesthood. I liked the place a lot and still do. I try to get back every year. They always strive there to include all types of backgrounds, to give individual attention where necessary, especially for those who have been away from academics for a long time. We had a lot of guys who had a high-school background only, and other guys with extensive education, very sophisticated intellectually. So they always tried to strike a balance. Seminary training tended towards favoring the more intellectually inclined, I believe, during the years I was there. I don't think that was bad, necessarily, but it was difficult for those guys who had been away from academics for a long time.

My late vocation is not as late as most others. In fact, many used to laugh because they were fifty to sixty years old, and I started out at a mere twenty-eight. But I always felt comfortable with those men. The association has made a different life for me, no doubt. For one thing, I have close clergy friends all over the country, even one in Australia!

The Church hasn't done much with second-career priests to date, probably because it hasn't taken the time to look at it yet. I think they'll find, more and more, that these late-vocation seminaries are producing very well. I think the word is out. It's just a matter of spreading the word, that's all.

I think the majority of second-career priests bring a fair amount of maturity that isn't necessarily guaranteed in a priest of the first career. While that may not hold up under close scrutiny, it's what I've observed. I think most of these men have made up their minds with a high degree of certitude. In many cases, they are fellows for whom the question of marriage has probably finally been determined without any problems. They realize that they will not likely get married. And they've had a chance to look at other opportunities and other experiences in their lives.

For me, I didn't have the pressure to get married that a lot of people have — to get out of the house or set off on your own. I had seen that in other families, but there was never any pressure on me ... mainly because my brother and sisters had not married. It's a rare family in that respect. We drew very close together when our parents died, and we've stayed that way. During high school and college, I did the normal amount of dating, and after that I had a pretty normal social life. I met a lot of fine young women who were ready for marriage, but I never really met one that I wanted to establish a permanent relationship with. So I've never had a problem with celibacy, and I pray that I never will. I seem to be fitting into the role pretty well. I have no major problems or fears that I know of. I hope it stays that way.

I don't see my work and involvement here in Kankakee to be any kind of sublimation. But, of course, I am totally involved. Besides the King Center and the other programs, there are my duties as associate pastor here at St. Stan's. Father Mike Sawlewicz, the pastor, says the daily Mass. During the winter we have it over at the convent because there is no sense heating up the church when there are only half a dozen or so people there. But I say Mass during the week at four different senior citizen residences, and then one day at a convent of sisters down here.

This is a parish with a lot of warmth to it, and people feel a close, personal contact with it. We get people from all over the area because of a combination of things: what we're saying in our homilies, the tone of the liturgy, the ethnic background, the warmth that is here. Father Mike's personality is responsible for most of this, I'm sure. Also, there are a lot of people who used to go to school here and now live in other parts of the community, but still come here to church. And there are those who know of our relations with poor people and want to be a part of that.

I think the gathering together of the community is vital, even if it's a small number. We have a pretty standard liturgy, but at the same time there's a closeness to it, a real warmth. You don't have to get gimmicky to keep the people coming. They seem to identify with us quite well.

You know, the Catholic Church in the United States is by and large a white Church. There have not been that many activities involving minority groups, at least not until the fifties and the sixties. That's a historical fact, and you just have to accept it. There's no sense in being angry about it. I'm just not inclined to approach a problem that way. I'm more inclined to say, "Well, what can we do to rectify the wrongs and right the situation?"

You have to handle each particular case and each individual person you deal with in its own terms, his or her terms. And you still use the general principles of the Gospel, just as you use the general principles of law. But you have to deal with reality. You can't be far out, or you become eccentric and lose your effectiveness.

My law background has been a great benefit to me. No doubt about it. The study part of it, the human relations, the exposure to the world — those are just immense foundations no matter what field I would have chosen subsequently. And since I've been in Kankakee and involved in this kind of work, it seems I've had a lot more technical legal problems come my way. Such things as real estate questions, zoning problems, contracts, grants, finances, and the legal problems of people in the parish. It's pretty widely known that I'm a lawyer, and people do come to me for legal advice. The way I handle it is not to practice law as such, though I still have my license, but to advise up to my limitations and then refer them to somebody else when the legal problems are too complex.

I'm not sure why I couldn't be doing the things I'm doing without being a priest. I probably could have gone in other directions, but that's not how a vocation works. I mean, I believe you are attracted into the place where you are called; and this is where I'm called right now. There are a lot of other professions, including the law, where there are great opportunities for social service, but this is the direction I chose.

I think service will continue to be the key in the future. One way or another, I think I will stay involved with minority groups. It might be in a traditional parish situation, but one that would have involvement with minority people. Maybe it'll be something else. But I feel confident that, being a priest, I will always be able to approach situations that I would never otherwise get involved in. That's the nature of the priesthood.

ROBERT MORRISSEY

A Priest Looking for a New Ministry

"When I was a kid, there was a young priest in my parish, Father Eugene Donnelly. He was a very quiet man, but he did a lot of things that I eventually found out about. There was a family with an acute alcoholism problem, and the cops were always coming around. Well, this priest knew the situation, and he would get the kids in the family off the street and take them swimming or bring them places. He was like that: he knew what was happening. He had a blue station wagon, and he'd take the kids and do something with them. A beautiful guy. I found myself thinking of him today because, here I was, driving a blue station wagon and I had a pile of kids in the back; and I thought, 'Hey, I've heard this tape before.' "

Father Robert Morrissey is fresh in from Vermont, where he has taken ten high-school kids on a skiing trip during their winter break. Dressed in a green sweater and with his brownish-red beard closely trimmed, Morrissey doesn't look much older than those kids.

He's thirty-four years old now and associate pastor of St. Mary's Church in Greenwich, Connecticut. That's one of the wealthier towns in the string of commuter communities northeast of New York City.

Corporations — and corporation executives —, are moving out here, and wealth is so common that many high-school kids go off to far distant places during their winter break.

Morrissey grew up in Whitestone, Long Island, New York, a dozen miles from New York City, where there were open spaces. "We had rabbits and all kinds of woods," says Morrissey. "And we used to burn down fields every year to play ball." He's still very close to his family: his parents and two older brothers and a younger sister, all of whom are married.

Like many men who entered the priesthood relatively late in life, Morrissey had once started, but then stopped, seminary training. He wondered whether it was really meant for him. Then he found a career in the challenging work of prison reform. After a while the thought of priesthood came back to him.

Obviously, Morrissey is a man who questions. Though happy in his priesthood, he feels restrained by the parish structure and longs to work more directly with people. He wonders whether there isn't a better way to find the closeness to people that he admired in the priests he knew in his childhood...

It's that kind of a priest, one like Father Donnelly, that I want to be. Someone who is aware that each person is special; that at times there are people who have particular struggles and — if you're sensitive, if you understand how to communicate — you can touch them and help them through their struggles.

And I think the kind of priest I want to be is simply a man who lives his faith, who shows that faith to others, not by what he says, but by his actions. And people will respond. People respond to you when you go to a hospital or visit them in their homes. When you go out to them.

It means a lot to me when people respond. It gives me more courage to go on. I want to be loved; I need to be loved. Like when I came in today, there was a lot of mail — notes and things — but there also was a little package. Somebody had sent me something for Valentine's Day. Little things like that mean a lot to me. Or if somebody says to me after Mass, "That was a helluva good talk," or gives me some feedback.

The most important thing for me is the Mass. I remember, when I was ordained, the bishop gave me a little sacramentary, a miniature of what we have on the altar. I opened up the cover and on the inside he had written, "May the Mass be always your joy!" That really touched me. There have been some days, boy, when it's been tough to get my ass out of bed in the morning; there have been times when I haven't felt like saying Mass, especially after being out on an emergency in the middle of the night. Sometimes I haven't felt like I had the energy to do it. But, you know, when you're doing it the way it should be done, it's the most powerful prayer. There are times when you have to struggle with it. To me, the Mass is the center of my life. If I can bring people to that — because that's where Christ touches us the most deeply — I believe I'm at my best.

I can remember in grammar school when the sisters used to encourage us to make a visit to Our Lord in the Blessed Sacrament. And I did. I used to bring my baseball glove and my bat, and I'd sit in the back of the church and I'd look toward those flickering candles and I'd say a prayer. But, you know, that little innocent thing was just what the Lord was looking for.

And, inevitably, who would be in the last pew? — Father Donnelly, saying his Office or just sitting quietly. He always spent time before the Blessed Sacrament. I do that now.

Since I've been a priest a few years, I find the interesting thing — I didn't understand it at that time, but now I do — is the relationship I had with the priests and the sisters. They planted the seed and, because my parents had a strong faith, it grew. My mother was a daily communicant, and my brothers and I served Mass. And the priests we had in our parish were there for many years. They had a really good relationship with the people. Really, it was like a family. We knew the priests; they watched us grow up. You had the feeling that you belonged. I don't see that kind of feeling of identification today in our parishes. I'd like it to be there. Very few young people associate with the parish church anymore. There are too many alternatives, and their faith is a different kind of faith, more a question of wanting the Church to relate to them rather than them relating to the Church.

When I was growing up, we lived five blocks from the local Catholic church, so it was the center of our focus ... like Andrew Greeley talks about the Church of the immigrant experience. Ours wasn't an immigrant family; my parents were born here. And my grandparents. But my great-grandparents were born in Ireland. Both sides. We were very much linked to the Church, my brothers and sisters, and all of us went through eight years at St. Luke's, the parochial school.

It seems to me, kids today, at least in this town, have so much money and things, and everyone caters to them. Because of that, there's really no need to associate with the parish. Whereas, in the past, you know, the Catholic experience was such that ... well, we had to stand over against the society in which we lived. Catholics saw themselves struggling to keep their identity. We had parish-sponsored activities for every age-group. Now we don't want that identity anymore, we don't need it, and Catholics have made it; so we've lost identification with the parish.

It seems to me the Church has to do other things. I was watching the news last night. Cesar Chavez and the whole lettuce boycott was on. That, to me, is where the Catholic Church in this country is making a powerful statement. And I got a letter today from one of my very best friends, who's a priest in Tanzania. He's working in many different mission stations. To me, that is where the Church is making a difference. Or take a guy like Father Bruce Ritter, a Franciscan who is working on the Minnesota Strip in New York, Eighth Avenue and Forty-fourth Street, salvaging young lives, both boys and girls, kids who are being brutalized by the whole prostitution scene. That's where our presence is being felt and making a big difference.

I think Catholics have been absorbed by our American culture. We've lost our spiritual roots. I don't think it's a very exciting time for the Church. I think it's a sad time because we've lost a lot of enthusiasm and a lot of people, including potential priests. I personally think it's like trench warfare right now, and I'm just trying as a priest in a city parish to lead people from a sense of isolation to a sense of genuine community where Christians really care about one another.

136

For me, it was a long road to the priesthood, When I was in high school, I was attracted to the Graymoor Friars. I was interested in their ecumenical work and felt drawn to their apostolate. So when I was seventeen, I went there for a year. But I left. It was a combination of things. I had unresolved feelings about my family, particularly my father, because he was an alcoholic at the time, and I could never really settle down ... you know, put my mind to it.

Then I went to college for a couple of years at Cathedral College in Brooklyn. Taking the bus and the train each day was an education in itself. But I was still having these struggles, academic and emotional, so I dropped out and got a job as an orderly in one of the local hospitals. Just kept myself busy. I heard about a place in Massachusetts where you could take Latin and Greek — Latin was important then. So I went there, and I really enjoyed it. I started settling in, and I did well academically. It was run by the Benedictines. I remember the prior saying that I really should stay, but I said I wanted to be a parish priest.

Well, then I went to Resurrection College in Kitchener, Ontario, which was fine, but it was really cold there; and then I finished up my college at Sacred Heart University in Bridgeport. The diocese started a seminary program there. I really enjoyed the atmosphere and got involved in the establishment of the first University Senate. After that, I did one year of theology at St. Mary's Seminary in Baltimore.

By this time I was doing all right academically. I felt I had proven to myself that I could do what I wanted to do. There was still that emotional part, though. I was resolving the problems with my family, but the thing I hadn't resolved was my sexuality. I said: "Gee, I don't think I can be a priest. I think I want to enjoy sex and marriage." I thought it was too much to give up. I didn't just discover this, it just caught up with me. Suddenly I realized what I was getting into. I said, "I think I'd better get out." When I left, they didn't think I would ever come back to the seminary. I figured I would be a good layman: I'd love people, do something good, be a social worker or something like that. I'd have a family ... the good life.

Through some people I knew, I got a job in state government in Connecticut. It was with an agency that was very political, very powerful, but one that had tremendous possibilities for good. It was called the Governor's Planning Committee on Criminal Administration. I became a planner. Basically, what I did was analyze situations and come up with programs and financing that would help improve the criminal justice system, in both a juvenile delinquency and an adult correction context.

This pushed me into a whole different world. I really saw the insides of prisons and correctional institutions. This was after the Attica riot in New York State, and things were very tense in our system too. Basically, prisons are warehouses. Nothing good happens in prisons. Everyone in the business knows that they don't work and that the best route to go is to try and get the people back into the community as soon as possible. Probation, parole — that kind of thing, you know. That works. But there's this tremendous fear ... you've got to lock everybody up. I sat in on enough parole board hearings to know that the really bad people, the psycho people — you can tell who they are. So you keep them locked up and the community is safe. The rest of them need minimal supervision. The most effective therapy is to return them to their families and help them get a job. Most of them want to make it.

Some of the programs I initiated are still working and doing very well. One of them I set up was an ombudsman program for the state prison. I felt very strongly that what happened at Attica shouldn't happen again. So I met with the corrections people — the commissioner and all his staff — and after a year of study and preparation, the program was established. Now there is an impartial observer who has access to the prison twenty-four hours a day. He can receive complaints and investigate grievances so that things don't get out of hand.

One time I went into one of the jails as a prisoner for five days. In Connecticut we have a unified system. The jails are called Community Correctional Centers and they're run by the state, not by county sheriffs. Well, I wanted to see what it was like in those places because I knew zilch about jails and I felt if this is going to be my career, I wanted to learn how it felt to be an inmate. So it was arranged. The people at the jail received me as an inmate convicted for possession and sale of controlled drugs. I was fingerprinted and everything.

It was an indelible experience. I don't want to go through it again, but it really helped me. First of all, I felt shock and then utter horror because of the way I was treated. You're dehumanized. They really put you down — you're stripped of your identity. And then, to know that you have the scorn of society ... the feeling that there's a real darkness. You go within yourself, you get depressed very quickly.

You become very sensitive to every movement, every sound. At the end of the tier when the guards slam the metal doors behind them, it is so final, so terribly deadening. I used toilet paper and a pencil I had stolen. To keep my sanity I set down my thoughts. And I counted the bricks on the wall ... or the bars. Just tried to find something to focus on.

And I knew I was getting out!

I began to see that quality of the people operating the prison system — especially the guards — is so critical for the inmates. They're the real therapists. It's the way they treat the inmates, day to day, that can help or harden them.

It made me very determined to try to improve the system. I really got into the work after that experience because I was motivated. It made me really aware of the direction we should be heading — beefing up probation and parole, and at the same time doing something diagnostic for inmates.

I audited courses in criminal law at the University of Connecticut at West Hartford and was thinking about going into law school and criminal law full time. There were all kinds of possibilities ... and, really, at that point in my life, I began to move away from the institutional Church. I stopped going to Mass, temporarily, and I began to go the route of the cocktail parties, the fun times. This was my wild period. I lived and worked in Hartford then. So I went that route, and I had a lot of fun — but it caught up with me. I ended up feeling defeated and guilty.

On my job, I was locking horns with the bureaucracy, seeing

all the things that could be done but weren't being done. They had the facts before them, but they were afraid to make decisions. I began to be unhappy with it, and at the same time I began to wonder where I was going with my life, what I was doing. I was about twenty-six and didn't see a future in it.

In the midst of that, I picked up *The Seven Storey Mountain* by Thomas Merton. I had read it in high school, but it just didn't affect me much then. But Merton's book, at that time in my life, was very important. And then I read other things by Merton. I was struck by his commitment to social justice and serving the real needs of people ... serving Christ and making the faith a living, vital thing. All of that kind of haunted me, and the idea of the priesthood came back very powerfully.

So I got in touch with the bishop, who had been aware of what I had been doing. Then I heard about Pope John Seminary and got in touch with them. And I went for their tests and interviews and they accepted me. And because I had theology before, I did the four years in three.

One of the things I'm grateful for as a priest is that I studied at Pope John. It was the launching pad for my second start and helped put a lot of things together in my life. The staff there was so wonderful. That whole experience gave me a sense of belonging and affirmation which I hope will carry me through my whole priesthood.

And I do love the priesthood. I love the people. It's just that I don't feel that this is the right mix. Something is missing from the recipe. You come out with all kinds of ideals, with good theology and spirituality, and then you're with priests and people who are just imbedded and rooted in the old ways. It's like Vatican II never happened. This is my second parish. The first was a parish with a priest who was very difficult to live with. It was a high-pressured parish, big, a lot of programs, and just the two of us. I was doing my thing and he was doing his thing. There was no togetherness at all.

One of the things that defeats us is that we're not really aware of the people around us and what their struggles are. We're isolated. We don't know anybody. Christ never meant us to lock ourselves into the maintenance of buildings that drain our resources. He told us to travel light. I just know, from my own experience as a priest, where people do respond. Look at all the spirituality that's happening all around us. It's not happening in the traditional parish structure. People are responding to things like Marriage Encounter, cursillo, and small groups where they can share their struggles and joys with others. People need spirituality that can help them get through the day's work; they are searching for a community of faith that will sustain them in an unchristian world.

Pastoring means, to me, being for people, trying to reach out, trying to understand what their struggles are and trying to relate them to the God that created them and redeemed them. I think the thing that I'm looking for is kind of like ... well, we all come from families, right? And this is where I can go back to my sister's death, because that had a profound effect on my life and my priesthood.

Elizabeth was a nursing student, twenty years old, a very beautiful girl with long brown hair. Being the baby of the family, we all kind of fussed over her. While studying for her RN, she was also working part time as a waitress and living with our parents in Queens. One Sunday night she left work, took a cab home, and stopped at one of the local disco places where her friends would hang out. She was looking for her friends, but they were at a rock concert in the city. So she walked to another place a short five blocks away, and that was the last time she was seen alive.

She was abducted ... you know, somebody grabbed her. For two months we didn't know what happened. It's still an unsolved murder.

I was at Pope John Seminary then, and I went home. My two brothers and I combed every neck of the woods, talked to every person we could — every bus driver, every cab driver — day and night. We came up with very little, but we found out how vulnerable all kids are today to a culture that promises more than it really delivers. She was young and trusting, and seeking the same thing we're all seeking — love.

It was a terrible struggle. For those two months it was a real hell. Finally they found her body in a completely different direction from where she was last seen, in a swampy field where there was a lot of high grass. The coroner couldn't determine the exact cause of death, but he felt she had been strangled. There was nothing in her system that gave any sign of drugs or anything like that.

I gave the homily at her funeral. That was the most difficult thing I ever had to do, but God really helped me. I dwelt on Christ's last words on the cross: "Father, forgive them." I think that was very necessary because there were so many people who were angry and upset and vengeful. It was terrible — the darkest side of people came out. It was very bad. It was suppressed, but it was there. I used Christ's words: "Father, into Your hands I commend my spirit." I spoke about how we have to suffer like Christ in the pain and struggle of life and to surrender ourselves to God. In Christ, we will not be overcome; we will not be overwhelmed by evil. If we're one with God through Christ, nothing can hurt us.

Well, it's taken four years to see the light at the end of the tunnel. As a family, I think we were all angry with God at that time. I didn't express it too much to my parents because I thought they had enough to deal with. But I did express it to others — how angry I was, how hurt I was that this could happen to such a beautiful person. The only way I could resolve it for myself was to forgive, by accepting the words of Jesus. The other alternative would only lead to bitterness, hatred, and revenge. I still have sad moments. Not too often, but sometimes I'll see something on television or hear about a murder on a news program and I'll get upset. I even had to catch myself one night. The priests were talking about a kid who had been in trouble and got beat up on a train station in New York City, and somebody said that it served him right for being out so late at night. I said: "Excuse me. Nobody — *nobody* — deserves anything like that, ever!"

My family has changed for the better. One of my brothers who was an alcoholic has stopped drinking and has a beautiful

142

life now. My mother went into a deep depression after Elizabeth's murder, but she's coming around now. She's fine. My father doesn't drink anymore. And all of us are more supportive of one another.

My sister's death has brought us all closer together. We're more aware of how fragile we are and how much we need each other. We're on the phone to each other during the week. People say, "What's all this closeness?" Well, I really love my family — my brothers, my sister, and my parents. And I'm really happy because I'm only a half hour away from home.

Elizabeth's death has made me a better priest. I know my sister is with God and I miss her. But I see her in the people I'm ministering to. There's been a real sensitizing to what's possible with life and with people: what they go through; what it means to suffer; what it means to face uncertainty, doubt ... all of those things that tie us up in knots. It really created an empathy within my heart for people.

This is why I make myself available to kids. I go to the public and private schools here. I have a youth group that is doing a lot to reach kids. Once you get a reputation, people start calling you to do this, do that. On my own time, on my days off, occasionally I'll do retreats outside of the parish for high-school kids. It's my way of living out what I've learned from my sister's death. Just being a brother. I don't see myself as "Father." I just want to relax, be with people, share my faith with them.

I think the family is the number one disaster area. There are so many divorces, so many people estranged, so many kids with only one parent. And then the motivations, the competition, the consumerism... You can't get a kid to sit down and be quiet; and they have trouble relating to the old values their parents cling to. It's what you have and what I have... It's what you own that gives you a sense of worth. It's too competitive. The worst time of the year in this town is when the high-school kids are taking scholastic aptitude tests. The competition is so ferocious! It's like a collective nervous breakdown. They want to get into the best colleges. It's terrible, and it just flows from the parents and their need to be number one. The whole town, not just the Catholics.

And there's this consumerism. It's got its hooks into us and we don't realize it. You know everybody is so upset about the oil crisis. It would be the best thing that could happen. People would stay home and get in touch with one another. The parents aren't lacking in good intentions, but they don't spend enough time with each other or with their kids. Families are all over the place. To have a sense of family life, you need to spend time together. And these parents and kids are so involved in all kinds of activities that they are driven away from one another.

I really see a need for direct ministry to these people. We have little groups and are producing other things, but we haven't done that much ministry for family units. Now if somebody really had had his act together and could have ministered directly to my family when my sister died, maybe a lot of the pain would have been avoided.

One of the problems, both on a diocesan and on a parish level, is a multiplication of programs. You could spend every night at meetings. Maybe we should create fewer programs and do more direct ministry to families. See them at home. Do less here and go out more towards them.

What I'd like to do is go into the neighborhoods and have Masses in local areas. Get people who have common interests together. Let's help them come to a deeper awareness of Christ where they live, in their own neighborhoods. I'm struggling with this ... I'm not sure. I don't know what the answer is, but we need to experiment.

I've seriously thought about establishing a religious community. It would be basically lay people, maybe a priest or two and a nun or two. I'm weighing what the goal would be, what we would be doing. I think we still need parishes, but parishes that are not cold, impersonal, one-day-a-week meeting places. We have to have vibrant experiences of belonging to Christ and to each other.

Yes, I'm disappointed in some respects. We have a great message to bring to people, but I think the present structure of parish, for me, hinders community. It gets in the way of many good things happening.

But, you know, it's still not worth jumping out of the parish, because, I think, there's a great deal of good to be accomplished — through the ministry that I can perform for people, through bringing Christ to the people, through my personal contacts, through my homilies, and through everything I can possibly give them. That, to me, is so important and worth the sacrifice.

I'm a very complicated person. I get all wound up. But, then, I say: "Hey, it's not a problem, it's a challenge. Christ is here!"

I know sometimes, for my own sanity, I have to say, "Hey, stop!" So what I do is — on my days off sometimes — I go away. I have a piece of land up in Vermont and I go up there, take my dog, and get lost. I'd like to build a cabin ... just go there and be quiet. I love to be quiet. It's important for a priest to have a place of his own. Sometimes I go to New York City to a movie or visit a friend or go fishing. All these help me unwind.

You'd be surprised how my dog helps my prayer life. I have to take her out to run two or three times a day. That gives me a time when I can pray. When I say *pray*, I don't mean words; I just mean being with God, getting my battery charged up.

And those problems I had with sexuality ... well, I've learned to accept my feelings. I'm healthy, I have my feelings as a man; but it's my commitment. I don't go beyond certain limits because I know that would lead to a very one-way thing.

While I was working for the state, I fell in love with a gal and went out with her for a year. That was a really healing thing for me, a good thing to be so close to a woman. It was a tough time. I needed that kind of relationship, needed to be loved in that special way. After that, it's been much easier to accept celibacy. Well, hey, day to day, I don't think anybody has their act completely together. I've heard enough confessions to understand that.

If I had become a priest sooner, I probably would have been a robot. I would have been a very suppressed, repressed person. I never would have faced these other issues. Well, maybe I would have. But I just see too many priests who went right straight through the seminary and never did anything else.

I don't know yet how I'm going to live ten years from now, but I'm not worried about it. I really am confident that God is going to help me to do my best. I'm going to look for every opportunity to question, to see if I can bring things about that are needed. But I'm committed to the priesthood and to Christ; I want to do as much as I can. And while I'm in this system of parish, I'll work with it and do the best I can. I look forward to the day when I can be involved in a team approach to the ministry, and I pray that our Church will encourage it.

WILLIAM KENNEDY

An Adman Leaves Madison Avenue

"Once or twice since I've been ordained, people have said, 'You must have hated your work before!' I didn't. I loved my work. And I don't regret that I didn't start on the priesthood earlier. They were good years."

The statue of the virgin St. Agnes looks rather incongruous on East Forty-third Street in New York. It is dwarfed by the towering buildings nearby and stands starkly white against the debris on the street.

In the heart of the city, just east of Grand Central Station, the Church of St. Agnes is a small island of refuge. Here, Father William Kennedy is one of a dozen priests who are trying to bring God into a world of steel and glass.

Kennedy knows the area well. A priest for only ten years, he was formerly an advertising man a few blocks north, working for a time at the giant Batten, Barton, Durstine & Osborn and rising to become a vice-president at Ted Bates. He liked the work and had not even thought about the priesthood until one day when it became clear that that was what he should be doing with his life.

He was forty-four, but he abruptly left Madison Avenue — know-

ing that he would return to the city he loves in a new and dynamic role...

I love everything about New York — the vitality, the tempo. It's my town. I have the same feeling now that I did when I came here as a teenager on a visit from Buffalo.

I was born and grew up in Buffalo. Both of my parents had been in a sanitarium for tuberculosis, and they contracted it again after I was born. My mother died when I was three, my father when I was five or six. My mother must have known of the possibility of that happening, so they came to an understanding with some friends of theirs who ended up raising me. I called them my aunt and uncle, but they weren't — I guess my uncle was my second cousin. But, in any event, I was raised as their own. They didn't have any children of their own.

After high school, I worked in the accounting department of a business there, but I had the feeling that I would like to get into radio — not the talent but the business side of it. New York was where the heart of the radio industry was, and of course radio was very big then.

So I came to New York in 1942. In those days, to quit a job without another in sight, particularly moving to New York City, required a lot of courage on my part.

So this greenhorn boy from Buffalo went right to the NBC personnel department. The woman there was very helpful. She said they could probably find some kind of job for me somewhere, but it would pay very little. But she suggested I consider advertising, because that was heavily into radio, and she told me of an employment agency that specialized in advertising jobs. So I went over there and I got a job very easily because there was a war on.

The job was with Donahue and Coe. They're no longer in business, but at that time they specialized in movie advertising — Metro-Goldwyn-Mayer, Radio City Music Hall, and any number of other motion picture accounts. Because I had accounting experience, I started in that area but quickly moved over to what we call the media department. The media department selects the medium to be used and then goes out and buys either the space or the time for the ad. Since it was wartime, they couldn't get as much newspaper print as they wanted, so they went into radio heavily. I became what they call an assistant time buyer, one that went out and purchased the time for the advertisements.

I stayed there ... I forget ... two, three years. So I was into radio, except from an advertising point of view.

Then, about '46 or '47, after the war, they could again get as much newspaper print as they wanted, and the feeling of most of these movie advertisers was that newspapers were the prime medium and radio was sort of secondary. So they cut back. And, coincidentally, the aunt who had raised me was taken ill; so I went back to Buffalo. I stayed there about a year, during which time she died, and I came to the point where I had to get out and live my own life; and I knew my life was in New York. So again I pulled up stakes and went to New York.

I contacted several salesmen who had called on me from radio stations. This was like on a Wednesday. By ten o'clock Monday I had a job with Batten, Barton, Durstine & Osborn.

I was at BBD&O for about three years, as a time buyer. Salesmen would come from television stations, networks, magazines, newspapers, or whatever to see me and present their pitch on why we should use their medium. We represented the clients. It is up to the media department of an advertising agency to come up with a plan that recommends a budget of so much money for television, so much for radio, newspapers — or whatever — and how it is to be spread out nationally and locally. I worked on Bond bread, which I don't think is around anymore, General Electric ... several other accounts of that nature.

Well, after a while it seemed time to move on to bigger and better things and I heard of an opening at an agency called Ted Bates & Co., which is one of the large ones these days. I got that job and was with them thirteen years.

At Ted Bates I started as a time buyer, became what they call a media supervisor, which meant that I had buyers reporting to me, and then branched out into all media: magazines, newspapers, radio and television, outdoor — everything.

149

From the time I started until the time I left, I had quadrupled my salary. I became a vice-president. Well, that's nice, but there are a lot of vice-presidents in an advertising agency. I was really the second in command of the department at the time I left. At one time there were about two hundred people attached to it.

At Ted Bates I came specifically to work on the Brown and Williamson tobacco account, and I continued to work on that until I got into the supervisory capacity. Brown and Williamson was just bringing out Viceroy cigarettes in the 1950s. That was one of the first filter cigarettes. That business built and built and built. We actually had two brands because Kool cigarettes were made by the same company. Television was just coming of age, and it was all local advertising. We didn't go on the networks but placed advertisements for the cigarettes city by city as they were expanding.

The reason I liked it was that I was working with people. I think I've always had that ability to get along with people and that's one of the things I like about being a priest. In advertising, to find the right man for the right job was a challenge. And, yes, I had to get rid of people who weren't performing, didn't fit into the job. That was difficult — but not all that difficult because many times it was for the person's benefit. If they're not performing, maybe they don't belong in that particular job or with that particular agency. You had to be ... not ruthless but certainly very levelheaded about it, unemotional.

Advertising agencies, of course, are very competitive and there is a big turnover. For many reasons — particularly in the creative end of it — a person might get stale working on one account all the time. Perhaps he could move over to another account in the same agency, but frequently they would just go to another agency. To a lesser extent, that applies to the business end of it too, the media people.

Over and above that, advertisers frequently change agencies, again because they feel the agencies are getting stale on their account. When that happens, there's a cutback in staff. Another agency will get that account, and that agency will hire other people. So there's a big turnover. Once a year we get together for lunch, five or six people I used to work with, and there's only one still at Ted Bates. Unless you're really up at the top, it's a young man's business. It's just a fact of life.

I had an ulcer once because of the tension. There's no doubt about that. A client calls up, and — indirectly — he is paying your salary; so when he says jump, everybody has to jump. Brown and Williamson was located in Louisville, Kentucky, and there were times when I was down there twice in a given week. I don't know how many airplane trips I've taken to Louisville. We were down there very, very often. I remember once we worked the entire weekend, and then Monday flew to Louisville.

So I had the ulcer, but I said I would never work at home: "When I leave the office, from here on I'm cutting everything off." For a year I didn't drink, I did all the diet requirements, and I got over it. I said I'd never have one again, and I haven't.

You know, one of the newsletters from Pope John Seminary had an article by one of my classmates who said, "As long as I can remember, I wanted to be a priest." Well, I picked that up and I said, "I didn't."

I guess it was '64. Things were coming to a head in my department, and they weren't coming to a head the way I wanted them to, and it affected me. Not that I was going to be let go, but there was a ... situation developing.

And all of a sudden, just out of the blue, it became crystal clear to me what I should do: I should be a priest. Don't ask me how — it just happened and I knew it clearly. It wasn't a religious experience, the Lord didn't appear to me or anything like that. It just was very clear that this is what I should do.

Maybe I had thought of priesthood before, deep down in my subconscious. I don't know. But there were never any doubts after that crystal-clear feeling came. I was going to leave Ted Bates, no matter what, because of the situation there. But I wasn't thinking of going to another agency. Once this thing overtook me, it seemed to me exactly what I should do and what I must do. It was what God wanted me to do, and I had to see it through. That may sound all very ... I don't know what; but it just never entered my mind that it wouldn't work.

151

I guess for the last couple of years it seemed to me that this wasn't a rewarding kind of life. I was just living for myself. I knew that there had to be something giving more meaning to my life than just working in advertising and leading a pretty comfortable life. There had to be something more than that.

I suppose if I had married, it would have been different. But I hadn't. I was fairly close to marriage once, but I don't think it would have worked out.

I was very close to a Benedictine monastery, Mount Savior in Elmira, New York. I belonged to the Third Order and I frequently went up there because I was interested in good liturgy. Still am. I suppose in the back of my mind there had been the question of whether I should ever enter there as a monk. The trappings were very attractive — the Gregorian chant, the beautiful liturgy — but I knew myself well enough and said, "Well, no, that life is not for me."

When it became so clear to me what I should do, I went up there for a weekend and talked to one of the priors. He said: "Oh, by the way, there's this new seminary opening up for delayed vocations, called Pope John XXIII. It's in Weston, Massachusetts. Why don't you look into that?"

So I got back to New York, quit the agency, and wrote to the seminary. They said they were filled for the first year, which was beginning in September, but they would be happy to consider me for the following year if I went to a Latin school. In those days Latin was still a requirement. And there was a good Latin school, St. Philip Neri, in Boston.

That, without a doubt, was the most grueling nine months I ever went through in my life. They gave four years of high-school Latin in nine months. The fact that I even survived was, to say the least, miraculous.

I hadn't been in a classroom since high school, and the Latin did not take. I struggled through it, but for somebody of my age to read Caesar — there just didn't seem to be any point to it.

The school was started right after the war, when a lot of men coming out of the service thought they'd like to enter the priesthood. By then it was open to anyone, and I think the average age was nineteen. So here I was, entering a milieu of teenagers. That was trying. There was a residence, an old brownstone, and I looked at the director and I said: "I am forty-four years of age. I can't picture myself in a dormitory, can you?" He said they had a couple of single rooms. I said, "Put my name on one of them." So at least I had that. But it was just pandemonium ... you know, the kids, after hours. And the meals ... well, I shouldn't get into that; the school is no longer in existence. I remember coming home at Thanksgiving and having people say, "God! What's happened to you?" I'd lost weight. It was incredible.

But somehow I survived, and somehow or other the seminary accepted me. What Philip Neri did for me was get me back into the study habits, back into the scholastic books again — which made it much easier when I did enter the seminary. Pope John was great, and as good as it was then, it's infinitely better now.

Well, it's not quite true that I never had any doubts. When I closed the apartment — I was living on Seventy-ninth Street and New York Avenue on the East Side — I had to sublet it because I had a lease. But I put my furniture in storage because I was enough of a realist to say that if I came back, I'd need a place to live. And when I went away, I told very few people where I was going. I figured if it doesn't work out, I'd just as soon not let everyone know where I'd been. This applied to my bridge-playing friends. I was the only Catholic in the group. Well, I'd pop into town, call one of them and say, "Can you get up a game?" They were very curious. One or two of the fellows thought I was with the CIA or something. But, in a couple of cases, there was a suspicion of what it might be.

Finally — I don't remember if it was the third or fourth year — this one friend said: "All right, Kennedy, this is the moment of truth. Tell us what you've been up to." They were surprised. I still see them and play bridge with them. They all came to my first Mass after I was ordained in 1969, and they stayed for the reception — and then left to play bridge.

My first assignment was the Church of Our Savior, which is at Thirty-eighth and Park. That was sort of half business, half residential, and I was there two years. I liked it. Then the archdiocese said they needed me at the Church of the Epiphany, which is more of a traditional parish, with a school and everything, at Second Avenue and Twenty-second. I was down there four years. Then the head of the personnel board came to see me and said they really needed someone at Holy Family Church, a United Nations church on Forty-seventh Street. After two years I wanted a change and I came here. I served as a deacon here, so it was good to be back.

I wanted to be in a business parish. It's the milieu that I had been in before, and I have some empathy with the people who come to this church. It's kind of amusing, every once in a while, to see somebody whose face I remember from the business world. People come in on their lunch hour, or before or after work. They come to Mass or confession, then have to go back. I did that sometimes when I was working. Ted Bates was at Rockefeller Center, and I'd go to the cathedral sometimes on my lunch hour.

Most of our people come from the office buildings and businesses in the area. We have Tudor City, which is a big development over on the East River, and we have several apartment houses; but our big thing is the business community. We stretch from the East River to Madison Avenue, and maybe from Fortieth Street to Forty-sixth.

When I came here, I knew that Monday through Friday would be very busy, and they are. We have nine Masses here, and we also have a chapel, St. Christopher's, where there are five Masses daily. There are some two thousand people a day going through these churches. I thought weekends would be very quiet, but we have eleven Masses on Sunday, from one-thirty in the morning until seven at night. We get a lot of hotel workers, for example; workers from the *Daily News;* a lot of people from hotels — guests and so forth. And we get some tourists. Sometimes a sacristan will line up a family to bring up the gifts at the offertory, and that's nice because we have very few children here ordinarily.

On Ash Wednesday, you wouldn't believe the mobs of people. An awful lot of them for the wrong reason — they never go to church, but they think they have to come get ashes. We're always busy, but Lent is always more so.

It's very rare that we have a wedding or a baptism or a funeral. We don't do as much counseling as I thought we'd do — it's mostly in the confessional. I find a great satisfaction in the confessional. Generally, we can't develop a relationship with people because of the impersonal kind of situation we have here; but, boy, you sure can in the confessional! You can do an awful lot of good there. I like it. I try to put them at ease — after all, they're there to receive reconciliation from God, and I'm just the intermediary. Many penitents are so relieved not to find the austere, impersonal, judgmental kind of priest that's been known to be around.

I can find God in the heart of New York. The highlight of my prayer life is the liturgy. I've always been interested in liturgy and, to me, the highlight of a priest's spiritual life is the celebration of the liturgy. I find Him in people. Because this is a sacramental ministry that we're doing here. Of course, that's the primary ministry of every priest; but in the more typical parishes, there are other things as well.

My personal life of course has changed, but because I'm in the middle of the city, I'm still able to maintain a kind of relationship with friends I've known for many years. But with other groups of friends, well ... the relationship has sort of dwindled off.

You know, I'm still the same person I was before, but I'm doing different work. As I told my bridge-playing friends, I'm still Bill Kennedy.

JOHN STRINGINI

A Free Man Finds Real Freedom

"From my own life, I see the struggles students are dealing with, the questions they're asking themselves, the doubts that they have in their minds. I had to struggle with the same questions and doubts, and I continue to have them: What is the Gospel calling us to? What does it mean to be a true Christian? In dealing with these questions, I think we make mistakes sometimes, but that's okay as long as we continue with the struggle. Hopefully, there will be people in our lives who will help us find the answers. That is what I hope to be."

Looking at him — curly hair, mustache, Paul Newman-blue eyes — you think of John Stringini as being a macho type. You can picture him growing up on Chicago's tough West Side, messing around with his friends on the streets, paying so little attention to school that he was kicked out.

You can see him, later, running an office in the Loop, hustling business on the phone, taking clients out to dinner. And you can imagine him driving out of his singles apartment to pick up a date in his Thunderbird.

John Stringini does look like a macho type, and he did all those things. But when he describes the remarkable religious experience he had when he was twenty-two years old, he is a gentle man. And when he talks about why he wanted to be a priest, it is in terms of service and love.

After that religious experience, Stringini did start out on the road to priesthood, going through the college preparatory portion of the program. But he got no further because he had doubts that he really had a vocation.

Then he went into business, running an employment agency for seven years. It was a good, rewarding life, and he was successful at it. But the call to priesthood could not be denied and at the age of thirty-two, he entered a seminary. He didn't expect to go into a college atmosphere upon ordination, but he has found satisfying and challenging work at the Newman Center of Northern Illinois University at DeKalb...

I find students very challenging. They're not the type to accept an answer just because you've said it. They ask why. And after hearing what you have to say, they might say, "Well, I don't buy that." Which is a challenge.

But there's an awful lot of emphasis today on spirituality. In the dorms they have their own Bible studies, their own prayer groups, without any priest or religious leader. They take it upon themselves to get together and pray. It seems like they're very hungry for the word of God.

They're more vocal, too. They're more willing to share the word of God with their brothers and sisters. When I was growing up, to talk religion in the cafeteria, for example, just wasn't done. It was a private deal, something to do in your room.

Students today are extremely open. They're not uncomfortable in talking about the areas that were taboo when we were growing up — like sex. They accept their own shortcomings today. They'll say that they were living with someone for five years, or that they had an abortion, or something like that — not that they're holding it up as something to be proud of. They see that now as something wrong and they are willing to accept it. But they are willing also to talk about it.

I think the most important thing is to accept people where they might be. Let them know that you're not there to judge them or lay criteria on them that they have to live by. To accept them as people who are basically good, people who are loved by God. And then talk with them. Place before them ideals, the Gospel message; and help them, through the experiences of your own life and what you have to offer. You're not going to water down what you believe to meet them, but you try to bring them where you feel the Gospel is calling them. I wouldn't be scandalized or angry with anybody for any particular life-style they might be living. It's their life, really. I just try to bring them the message of the Gospel, and I hope to guide them to a more meaningful life.

I see my calling as priest to help people deal with the issues and to be there with them, letting them know that they are accepted and loved. God has gifted me with an ability to reach people. That's not egotistical. I just feel that if I really use that gift, I can really help people to grow. My satisfaction comes in knowing that God is working through me in that way.

I can identify with young people, and I can identify with old people. I feel very comfortable with all types of people. I haven't found any age-group that I don't enjoy working with. I have a way of making people comfortable, making them feel as if they'd known me a long time.

In my younger life, the feeling of wanting to show this acceptance of people, of wanting to be warm with people, was something I more or less stifled because it didn't fit the image I saw as manly. On the West Side of Chicago, peer pressure was very strong, gangs were very strong. In any kind of subculture like that, might made right. The one with the most respect was the toughest guy. So the image of being the hard guy, the tough guy, the person that doesn't show any emotions, was important. Very macho. The guys who were into books or didn't come with us, we identified as sissies.

I was born and raised in Chicago around Madison and Pulaski and went to Catholic grade school there. Catholic high school, too, for two years. After my second year, I was thrown out. I was the kind of guy who would keep getting himself in trouble: school wasn't my bag. I enjoyed just being out, being free. I was very much a gang type of kid, I liked being with my friends, I didn't want to be home. Being out in the neighborhood, doing nothing, was my idea of a good time. So when I was asked to leave high school after my second year, I couldn't have cared less. But my father insisted that I graduate from high school, so I went to Morton East in Cicero and graduated from there.

After high school, I didn't want to go to college. I just wasn't ready, but I didn't know what I wanted to do. My family wanted me to be doing something, so I went to barber college because a few of my friends were going. I got out of there and worked as an apprentice for a couple of years. That wasn't really what I wanted. I just didn't know what I wanted. I just wanted to be out, messing around. That's all I cared about, I didn't want to hear any hassle … you know?

Well, by this time I'm twenty-two years old and, you know, I was never a religious guy, even though I went to the grade school, the high school. I went there and I listened, but it went in this ear and out this ear.

One morning when I was twenty-two, I was getting out of bed and I stepped on a needle. It was too deep for the doctor to use a local in the office to take it out, so he put me in the hospital. Well, I was in the hospital for a couple of days. It was the first time that I'd been on my back for any period of time, at least for a long enough time for something to come through to me, because I was always on the go.

Well, I had a religious experience. Unless you've had a religious experience, it's hard to explain. Some of the people I work with in the charismatic movement here at Newman identify with what I'm saying, but I know it's hard for people who have not experienced this to understand. God touched me. It wasn't a vision or anything like that. It was just that I felt the presence of God in my life so strongly. I don't know … it just happened. It wasn't anything on my part. Strictly a gratuitous gift from God. It was almost like Paul on the road to Damascus. That complete turning around, that complete reversal of life-style.

I was totally changed. My whole attitude was different. At that moment I knew I wanted to be a priest. Priesthood! My God, with my background? I just wanted to be a priest; I was sure that this was what I was called for.

When I got out of the hospital, I started going to Mass and Communion every day. My family was just shocked. I just continued going and I decided to go see my parish priest. Now, I had never met the man. I introduced myself to him and told him what had happened to me and told him what I would like to be. And he thought that was fine.

He told me about a brand new seminary starting out in Lockport, Illinois, St. Charles Borromeo Seminary. The priest had a friend there and offered to write a letter to him. So I went there to meet that priest, who was a very spiritual, a very good man. He said that since summer was starting, I could take a couple of courses to see how I'd do. I was open to anything. So I went to St. Joseph's High School, took Latin, English, geometry, and creative writing. I was in there with freshmen! But it really didn't bother me; I was on a spiritual high. I could have been with grade-school kids and it wouldn't have made any difference.

So the priest said okay, I could go to Lewis University, which is next to the seminary. I did well there. I put in a lot of time, but studying came relatively easy to me there. I enjoyed what I was doing, and I graduated from there in 1969 with a philosophy major and a minor in physical education.

During my four years in college, I was on a spiritual high. Literally. I never had any doubts about my vocation. I spent an awful lot of time in chapel. I could eat, sleep, and talk religion.

Nothing in the world would bother, everything was enjoyable, I didn't find any fault. The whole world could collapse and I'd be smiling. If I saw something wrong, I'd say: "Well, that's okay. It's my responsibility as a Christian to accept it." In other words: if you can't say anything nice, then don't say anything. That sort of attitude. I was the perfect seminarian.

It was during the last part of my fourth year of college that I started to have doubts. Everything wasn't as clear. My sexuality started to become bothersome for me. Prior to that I never had a problem with that. Now I was starting to get aroused physically. I didn't know what was happening, and I took this to mean that maybe I didn't have a vocation.

I went to the rector and I said I wanted to leave, not go into the seminary. He was shocked. I was the last person in the world to expect that from. After graduation, I left.

I didn't know what I was going to do. But I went back to school to get my teaching certificate. I had three months before I could get an assignment to do my student teaching, so I took a job with an employment agency in downtown Chicago. It was dealing with finding jobs for males — engineers and so forth. I liked it, I liked it very much, and I did well at it.

When I got my call from the school where I was to do my practice teaching, the fellow who ran the employment agency — he was a young guy and we got along real well — said to come back to him after I'd completed that assignment. When I finally finished student teaching, he asked me to come downtown and talk over lunch. I had a job already offered to me by that time, running the physical education department at the seminary and teaching a humanities course in the high school. I figured I'd cut hair during the summer. At lunch he asked me how much I would want before I would take a job with him. I said $12,500 a year. He said, "You got it." I talked it over with my family and I figured I could always go back and teach, and I could always cut hair.

He asked me to work in the temporary end, dealing with women, getting them office jobs. Well, as a single guy, that appealed to me much more than dealing with men. So I went there and started working for him and I really enjoyed what I was doing and I was very good at it. I was soliciting over the phone, meeting people, getting business. I got a lot of business for him.

After a while, I saw that I could stay there and help that business or I could start my own, because I had a few dollars. I decided to leave. There was another fellow there, an Italian kid also from the West Side. We got along real well, so we figured we would give it a shot. We opened up an office on Dearborn and Randolph and were very successful.

We had a temporary-help service, Universal Services, Inc., and a full-time agency, Fox, Inc. I was there seven years. I enjoyed my work totally, and I loved the people I was meeting. And it was very rewarding financially. In the last couple of years I was making forty thousand plus a year.

I enjoyed my work, and I worked hard at it. Some people wondered how I could put in that many hours, but it was what I enjoyed doing. I'd get there about eight o'clock and I'd stay till five-thirty or six. I just wanted to make it big, I wanted Universal Services to be the biggest temporary-services agency in Chicago, and, believe me, there was a lot of competition.

I had what I wanted. Being a single guy and not having any overhead other than my apartment, my automobile, and so on, I had the life. If I wanted to go on a trip, I went. If I wanted to take off, I took off. I just had it. I'll admit that I like the finer things — nice clothes, expensive suits — so I had a lot of them. My job warranted dressing well, going to nice restaurants, taking vacations, driving a nice car, dating. I lived in one of those singles apartments ... you know, with the sauna and the pool and everything.

But I wasn't the playboy type. I was involved with the Church all this time, teaching CCD. I felt that commitment toward Christ. And even though I wasn't on that spiritual high anymore, every once in a while the idea of priesthood would pop into my mind again.

Look, I was dating and enjoying what I was doing. I was happy. I would get angry when this idea would pop up. I didn't want it. And so it would leave and I'd be very much into my job again; but then it would pop up again. I'd be dating someone I really cared for, and all of a sudden, zappo, here comes this crazy notion again. It was really frustrating. Or I'd see a priest and I'd feel elated again, that I had a calling to that, and it was absolutely beautiful.

So I struggled with those tensions, and in March 1972, when I was thirty-two years old, I had a heart attack. It was a major heart attack—twenty percent of my heart is damaged for life. The doctors couldn't understand it. I was a nonsmoker, I was in good shape, I exercised an awful lot. But I did dumb things too. I'd come home from work, eat, and then go right to the gym and exercise. There were all those things. It hasn't affected my life since, though. I have a very vigorous exercise that I follow now. I run two miles a day. I was running two and a half miles a day before. It was something that happened; it's gone, and I must continue to live my life.

Well, I was out about a year. But after I got better, I went into the seminary. This time it was Sacred Heart, in Milwaukee. I finally had to deal with it, I had to answer the call. It was always there. It's such a funny thing — when you have a calling, it's just constantly there. Oh, you try to turn away from it, but you just know it's right. You know it's for you.

So I had to answer it. I thought about it so much. I knew that it was my decision. I enjoyed dating, and I felt that I could have been very happily married. I could see myself in that role very easily. I could have had my employment agency and been a very good Christian person. But I don't think I could ever have reached the type of relationship with Christ that I was being called to.

The priesthood isn't for everyone, of course. I think everyone's vocation, whether it be for a police officer, a teacher, or anything else, is very sacred because that's what God wants that person to do.

And I believe it started when I had that religious experience at the age of twenty-two. I have had a relationship with Christ in a very personal way since then, which, I believe, has called me to the priesthood. It's gone through many different phases, but it's getting deeper and deeper.

But I am different than when I was on that spiritual high. I'm much more realistic, very much a part of the real world. As I said, nothing in the world would bother me at that time. It was like being on a holy card. I really didn't belong on earth, I belonged with the angels. I really was up there somewhere. My relationship with Christ has changed. For four years I was in a kind of ecstasy. My relationship now is a truer one, one in which I feel what it is to suffer with Christ — to say no to myself.

My sexuality, for example. Before, a young lady could come in front of me and disrobe, and, I suppose, I'd smile and say, "Poor child." I could care less. Before, in four years in college, I never once had any thought of females, never once had any physical arousal. My sex was more or less repressed. I wasn't even conscious of it.

Now, my sexuality is very much a part of me and I am aware of it; but because I've chosen a different life-style, I can deal with it. I am very much attracted to what is out there, but I have to say no to myself because of what I am called to be: a priest leading a celibate life.

The hardest thing to give up was knowing that I could never have a relationship with a woman, a sexual relationship. To be a celibate, to say no to that, to feel that I could never have children of my own; on days when I'm frustrated, not to be able to come home to a woman and have her love in a very human, physical way which would express our much deeper love — for me that was the hardest thing. It's ... a loss. When people lose a son or a daughter, they have to go through a process to deal with that loss. Well, that was something I had to deal with, the loss of my sexual life. Sure, I'm sexual, in the sense that I'm myself; but I can channel that in another way. But not being able to express it in the way people usually express it ... well, that was a loss.

It's only through the grace of God that one can survive in this calling. To be a priest in our situation means to be celibate; and if God is calling me to the priesthood, the grace of a celibate priesthood is also given. So I have to cooperate with that grace.

But sexuality is still going to be a strong desire. But by learn ing to channel it — by working harder on a homily, for example, or by spending more time in relationships with people, or by spending time in prayer — there is that energy you get. You use the grace in a very Christian life and in a constructive way ... to help people and to develop your own talents.

And you understand what it was for Christ to suffer and to give up His life on the cross. Because each time you say no to that, you die a little more to yourself. No, it's not "normal," but Christ said He was a contradiction and the world wouldn't understand. And people don't understand. They ask: "Don't you like girls? Are you homosexual? Are you crazy?" You try to tell them, but they don't understand. They can't get it.

I'm still struggling with this, but I know that when you have a love affair with Christ, that just takes care of your relations.

I don't have any doubts about my vocation. I know I'm called to be a priest. But, sure, there are doubts in the sense that you really don't know if you're going to be able to do it all the time. You see those guys who have left, a lot of them better than you are. What happened? Are you going to be able to go through it the rest of your life? Are you going to be a good priest?

Why did I want to be a priest? The more I'm into it, the more that question clarifies itself. To me it's basically a question of service. I want to be of service to people, to help people to come to know Christ, to help society become the place that the Gospel is calling it to be; and to show that, though the human situation is one of suffering, there is hope because Christ has called us to resurrection.

I hope I'm a good priest. I hope I am an understanding person. I hope I can be very compassionate towards people and really empathize with what they're struggling with. I don't really care too much if I'm ... Well, some people talk about brick-and-mortar men; I'm not too interested in that. A successful priest, to me, is one who is faithful to what he is called to; and I think I am called to be a servant for the people, to be a witness for Christ, to be a proclaimer of the Word. I want to be humble enough to see where I'm at fault and need some growth, and I want to be willing to take criticism from people. Just being myself.

I am no different from any other man: I have my weaknesses, I have my shortcomings, I am as human as anyone. But I'm called to a way of life, a special way. It is a calling, a gift given by God. So you say: "Lord, I know You're calling me. I'll do my best. Just give me the graces."

Sometimes I think about what kind of priest I would have been if I hadn't dropped out that first time. I'm just speculating, but who knows? — without having that experience, and then the experience of working, who knows what troubles I might have had in the priesthood? If I had gone into the priesthood after that first experience, I don't know how I would have dealt with some of my own needs.

Having all those material things, having dates, being free, being young, being my own boss — having all that and then opting for the priesthood helped me, I think, to deal with the same kinds of things that come up in priesthood. The energy that I was exerting making a buck is now exerted toward helping other people to know Christ and toward helping myself get into a better relationship with Christ.

I think life is a relationship with our Creator and the phases we go through are just phases in that relationship. I went through many phases. Now, working with students here at Newman, finding myself in the priesthood, I'm in another phase.